# THE CREATIVE WORLD OF MOZART

# THE CREATIVE WORLD

## OF

## *Mozart*

### Edited by PAUL HENRY LANG

The Norton Library

W · W · NORTON & COMPANY · INC ·

NEW YORK

First published in 1963 by arrangement with *The Musical Quarterly,* in which the chapters originally appeared.

W. W. Norton & Company, Inc. is the publisher of current or forthcoming books on music by Putnam Aldrich, William Austin, Anthony Baines, Philip Bate, Sol Berkowitz, Friedrich Blume, Howard Boatwright, Nadia Boulanger, Paul Brainerd, Nathan Broder, Manfred Bukofzer, John Castellini, John Clough, Doda Conrad, Aaron Copland, Hans David, Paul Des Marais, Otto Erich Deutsch, Frederick Dorian, Alfred Einstein, Gabriel Fontrier, Harold Gleason, Richard Franko Goldman, Noah Greenberg, Donald Jay Grout, James Haar, F. L. Harrison, Daniel Heartz, Richard Hoppin, John Horton, Edgar Hunt, A. J. B. Hutchings, Charles Ives, Roger Kamien, Hermann Keller, Leo Kraft, Stanley Krebs, Paul Henry Lang, Lyndesay G. Langwill, Jens Peter Larsen, Jan LaRue, Maurice Lieberman, Irving Lowens, Joseph Machlis, Carol McClintock, Alfred Mann, W. T. Marrocco, Arthur Mendel, William J. Mitchell, Douglas Moore, Joel Newman, John F. Ohl, Carl Parrish, Vincent Persichetti, Marc Pincherle, Walter Piston, Gustave Reese, Alexander Ringer, Curt Sachs, Denis Stevens, Robert Stevenson, Oliver Strunk, Francis Toye, Bruno Walter, J. T. Westrup, Emanuel Winternitz, Walter Wiora, and Percy Young.

ISBN 0 393 00218 7

PRINTED IN THE UNITED STATES OF AMERICA

4 5 6 7 8 9 0

# CONTENTS

49301

# ILLUSTRATIONS

# THE CREATIVE WORLD OF MOZART

# INTRODUCTION

## By PAUL HENRY LANG

It may be said that there are composers who develop by constantly stepping out of their frame and following a new direction. Because they continually uproot themselves they grow erratically and may perhaps fail to attain their full stature. Others circle their domain with their first steps; every circle brings them to known territory, yet every circling results in new discoveries and conquests.

Mozart was of the second type; he was always faithful to himself. Even in his early works most of the "themes" of his music are already present, and it is fascinating to watch how these "themes" reappear in successive works, always deepened and enriched. Such a composer does not constantly seek the new, trying to "advance"; he holds his ground ever more firmly, becomes stronger; every new work means more than the previous one precisely because he is content to follow his natural growth. To change, and to proceed into new territories, is always an adventure; for the creative artist the only sure progress is into the depths of his own soul. And this is the most difficult and most exciting road.

*    *
*

Musical language is born before the ideas it will express. Mozart, too, began his career as a competent user of the musical language and very soon handled it with the skill of a virtuoso. We may recall that the early poems of Goethe also give the impression of exercises in style, and like him, Mozart early acquired discipline in a rigorous school. This discipline soon taught him the emptiness of external virtuosity and he yearned for a different kind of virtuosity, greater and more difficult than the mere handling of the idiom. His youthful voice is tender and discreet, but it has a definite character; the well known clichés of the idiom acquire an individual charm and the thrice familiar turns become in some incomprehensible way personal. In the hands of any one of his journeyman contemporaries these melodies and motifs are commonplace; when Mozart uses them they become human wisdom. The most important utterances of poets and musicians, from Homer onward, have always been these commonplaces made their own. To rediscover the commonplaces and to dare to use them in one's own way requires more courage and judgment than to seek for novelty at any price.

Still, this personal tone does not entail anything extraordinary or bizarre; on the contrary, there have been few great composers whose music was so intimately and organically tied to that of his predecessors as Mozart. Actually, one might call him a conservative, but a conservative who is fresh and unspoiled. This is an untouched youth, eyes alight with the first ideals. His idealism can remain conservative for it is intimate and as yet unexposed to reality; there is nothing with which it can conflict. Revolutionary art is born where the ideal is in conflict with experience. But the young Mozart's music did not concern itself with external reality; there was no rebellion in him, at most he sighs but this sigh fails to become concrete in his music for some time to come. Even when in Paris, in the fascinating bustle of the metropolis, he stands apart, like a wondering child whose dreams walk in purer and higher regions. This music originated before mankind had fallen into sin, it is angelic musical poetry, perhaps like the poetry of Shelley. But if Shelley is an angel with a sword, Mozart is an angel with a harp, though his wings are equally powerful.

*     *

*

The elements of Mozart's greatness are beyond analysis and discussion. Other great musicians can be discussed, but his music does not offer any opening — it is pure, unbroken, finished to the very end. There is no such harmonious phenomenon in the entire history of music. Baudelaire's famous *mot*, "guileless poet," fits him, for indeed, he was guileless and straightforward, faithful to his vocation, which was to create beauty from such matter as happens to be, from the little and sad matter of our own life. How many things determine this life! But the composer transforms them into noble beauty which rises above the circumstances and remains, like the coral palaces, even after those who gathered and built them have gone. And he does it not so much consciously as with the instinct of the coral animals. This is the true and ancient instinct of the creative artist. It lived in him, creating the individual world of a peculiar beauty, both happy and tragic, formed from life, yet higher than life; for Mozart's poetry is always the highest lyricism, akin to the beauty of classical Greece even when he sang of frivolous barbers and swashbuckling adventurers.

This noble and guileless musical poetry, this pure creative greatness which remained untouched by the disorders of life, was looked upon as a miracle by posterity, which did not understand the composer's personality. It is sad to contemplate that this music was created by a composer who himself was not quite of this life, who always was a guest, one of us but not quite belonging among us. Not that this saint of song did not warmly feel the world — he was tied, like all of us, with a thousand threads of desire and love to this earthly life. But the desire abandoned the struggle and the love became that of the wanderer who gladly sits down to our table but knows that he cannot stay for long.

Perhaps earthly things were more interesting and sad to him because he knew he was to leave them, or perhaps they seemed not so serious and sad to him as they seemed to others. It was easier for him to make beauty out of them. His was not a combative life but a contemplative one. How fantastic must life appear to him who looks at it so to speak from the outside, as at a strange exotic country, in which to live means squalor and sorrow, while to travel in it causes pleasure and nostalgia. It is this detachment that sheds a particular light on his music, on its perfection, sure and faultless composition, technical virtuosity, and infallible control. There is a certain single-minded determination for perfection in every elaboration of line and detail that to the uninitiated appears as playfulness, and even the initiated may feel that at times this music is dictated less by necessary and logical progression from its beginning than by the playful joy of imagination. There is some truth in that, but if music ever had a Cellinian goldsmith Mozart was he.

Thus he went, pouring out his song and his strength, through the indifferent world towards his sure death. But on his way he opened up for us an entirely new world. His progress was not struggle but sorrow, and perhaps it was sorrow because it was not struggle. Every force can be vanquished except one: resignation. At the bottom of this brilliant and playful music there burns the warmth of a great suffering, a doomed love and desire for life that are warmer than life itself. Many a person outlives his love of life; only the creative artist is outlived by it. Now the goldsmith's delicately traced melodies, his beautifully chiselled harmonies receive a wonderful internal glow, and the glow fuses everything into great art. Thus the goldsmith becomes a great artist, beyond the accusation of playfulness. Here discussion ceases unless we are willing to question the very principle of beauty-creating poetry.

*     *

*

The soul has an ability to learn from another soul only what is its own, what is itself in another personality, somewhat as a magnet attracts its own kind of metal and leaves paper and wood untouched. Even the old contrapuntal forms, devices, and turns contained elements that suddenly became Mozartean; but somehow the severe lines end in personal phrases, the rhythm has a different mood, and in the midst of the most complicated part-writing there appear the simplest homophonic procedures, lightening the texture with a suddenness that may just as suddenly depart.

In Mozart's early works, some of which were virtual paraphrases of compositions of his elders, there is no plan or principle at work; art engrossed in itself flits from flower to flower. What was important to the youngster was to enjoy his own budding ability to handle the idiom. The new period began when he became convinced that every flower would not do, when he discovered that there are eternal flowers. The innocent pleasure in playing with models gave way to a desire to lay down serious principles, the principles of faithfulness to form and mood. Contemplating these later works, one is aware not only of what Mozart still retains from his heritage but of what he no longer uses. He is disciplined, never accepts what obviously offers itself, and prefers the nuance to the easy solution. His greatest triumphs are reached not in works that rest on a pregnant idea or on a single impulse, but in those where every secret lies in the details and manners that escape the unwary. So he advances to the wellhead of true art, never thwarted by difficulty, never compromising with current taste, and never disturbed by indifference met with. He is akin to the magician of the fairy tale who, sensing his approaching death, prodigally shakes out his bag of tricks. A young magician, and yet old and wise like all those to whom death is close.

It is of course romantic criticism that sees the creative artist through his fate, but it would be difficult to understand Mozart without this romanticism. Young death permeated his life, his ideas, his accents, colored his music. It was a young man who wrote to his father: "Since death, when we come to consider it closely, is the true goal of our existence, I have formed during the last few years such close relations with this best and truest friend of mankind, that his image is not only no longer terrifying to me, but is indeed very soothing and consoling!" He was lifted from our profane world, saved from further battles and mistakes, made wise, even transfigured, the poet of heroic resignation. Mozart did not beg for his life, he was acquainted with death.

Art arrests time. It continues life after death and illuminates the darkness. For Mozart art was the condition of life to which he could not be unfaithful, the strength, hope, and wealth of threatened life. He suffered from the lack of understanding for his art; the perfection he pursued interested few, perhaps only his devoted and wise old friend, Haydn. Success bypassed him, others less accomplished and less perfect attracted attention. This hurt him, but all this was a matter of time, the true content of his life was beyond time. To compromise his art would have meant the loss of his only hope, the secret health and security of a sick man.

We spoke of the guileless poet, and yet his greatness does not lie here. Creative greatness is not something so negative as guilelessness. It is not the absence of flaws that makes art great, not what is missing, but what is in it.

*     *

*

What a strange unfathomable thing, music! What is it that endows it with essence and value? Surely not content. We know well that great ideas are not sufficient for a great symphony; many a work that contains magnificent invention ends by being learned and naked. Could it be feeling? Hardly, for some of the warmest, most profoundly felt pieces are poor compositions. Perhaps form? Some of the most accomplished formal structures strike us as empty play with patterns. Or is it the sum total of all this? But experience has shown that any one of them may be missing and the composition may still be great. What, then? It is obvious that we are no more able to furnish an answer than the many thinkers from time immemorial who were equally baffled by this riddle. Only the hackneyed and much-abused word, magic, will be appropriate and we use it as the mathematician uses "x," the unknown, which cannot be named but at least can be indicated with a symbol.

*     *

*

The closer Mozart gets to his early grave the more he is absorbed in this magic even though the world is proportionately less interested in it. His music is no longer contemporary. With almost stubborn consistency he pares down everything "modern" and everywhere offers nothing but what for want of a better term we call pure classicism — the clarinet concerto, the divertimento for string trio, *Così fan tutte*. How incredibly happy this music of the magician ready to face death, offering the magic of a fulfilled life. Everything now is concentrated and telescoped. The intoxication of youth has not yet faltered when the first ideas of old age, far ahead of old age itself, add new subjects to the earlier themes. The composer begins to audit his life, to understand his fate and his destination. He looks at the cornucopia of his music, modestly, yet with pride. He thinks of death, too. He embraces music, the secret alchemy whereby he can create for himself joy out of misery. He holds on to music as to a lifeline, and in these last years pours out work after work without pause.

Perhaps every art should take its departure in this manner, like the sun throwing its most colorful rays in setting.

# MOZART'S CREATIVE PROCESS[1]

## By ERICH HERTZMANN

WHEN Mozart died, on December 5, 1791, he left his wife Constanze with two children, a considerable debt, a half-finished score of the Requiem (the fee for which had already been paid in part), and a great many music autographs. Because of the shock of his death Constanze had a nervous breakdown. After she regained control of herself and found that she was without any financial security, what would have been more natural for her than to liquidate the musical estate? But she did not do so. Constanze, who had been completely dependent upon her husband and who had not shown any talent for organization, not even for housekeeping, now turned out to be a good manager. In spite of her needs, she did not sell her husband's autographs, but instead she guarded them carefully and requested their return when she sold the publication rights to Breitkopf & Härtel and other publishing houses. Moreover, her friends, Abbé Stadler and Georg Nikolaus Nissen, the Danish diplomat who later married her and wrote a valuable biography of Mozart, made an inventory of all the manuscripts. Constanze also saw to it that the Requiem was finished by Mozart's pupil and friend, Franz Süssmayr, and subsequently delivered to Count Walsegg, who had anonymously commissioned it.

It was not until eight years later, in 1799, that, after bargaining with Breitkopf & Härtel, she sold the complete collection of musical manuscripts to the young Johann Anton André, who cherished it with great love and care throughout his long life. With this acquisition he also bought Mozart's autograph of his thematic catalogue, which listed all the compositions written between February 9, 1784, and November 15, 1791. A few years later, in 1805, André published this catalogue, in the preface to which he remarked: "It is most interesting to study his original scores, since one can best observe Mozart's first inspiration,

[1] An address delivered for the Mozart Bi-Centennial Festival at Columbia University, New York.

as well as the further development of his ideas." In a handwritten catalogue of all the manuscripts in his possession André gave more detailed information about Mozart's process of creation. His observations, though brief, show his awareness of and interest in this problem, and they have been quoted and elaborated upon by later Mozart scholars. Pertinent discussions about Mozart's creative process can be found in the standard biography by Otto Jahn, who also gathered a great deal of scattered information from earlier biographies and from memoirs of Mozart's friends and personal acquaintances. In more recent times, the late Alfred Einstein threw additional light on the problem in his numerous writings on Mozart, after he had re-investigated the available manuscripts for his new edition of Köchel's *Mozart-Verzeichnis.* In spite of all these excellent observations, only part of the veil that obscures the mystery of Mozart's creation has been lifted.

Further insight into the problem of Mozart's compositional technique can be gained from the investigation of other composers' works. A comparison of his autographs with those of Beethoven shows revealing differences in musical conception. In view of the tremendous musical production, changes in Mozart's autographs are rare. While Beethoven never ceased improving upon his work, Mozart, even if he made corrections, seldom touched the core of the music; at best his changes add finesse and niceties that can be scarcely perceived by the listener. Moreover, it is open to question whether they are always real improvements.

Beethoven left a great many sketch books, in which we can observe his mental struggles and the various stages of his compositional procedure, from the very first germ of a thematic idea to the finished form. There are no sketch books by Mozart in existence. Thus we have to gather our information from literary sources in his letters and contemporary memoirs, from scattered sketch leaves, from unfinished compositions, and from the final autographs of his completed works.

Constanze's reminiscences, which were published in periodicals shortly after Mozart's death, as well as other contemporary reports, abound in stories about Mozart's fantastic inventiveness and productivity. He was never short of musical ideas and, as Constanze put it, "he wrote down music in the same way as he wrote letters." Mozart could do so at any time of day or night; he was able to compose while playing billiards, of which he was so fond, or while traveling in a stage-coach. Nothing could distract him. A musical genius, to whom dearth of invention was unknown and who composed music continually, is faced with the problem of selectivity. It is amazing to see how sure Mozart is of himself when he works on a composition. His fertile and ingenious mind, one feels, solves any problem before he is aware of its existence. If more than one solution offers itself at the same time, he has no difficulty in making up his mind and takes his choice without hesitation.

Numerous anecdotes about his memory, his power of concentration, and the speed with which he composed have been recounted by all Mozart biographers. No doubt some of these stories are legendary, but others, especially those that Mozart relates in letters to his father,[2] cannot be doubted. Thus, on October 6, 1781, he reported to his father: "What would at other times require fourteen days to write, I could do now in four. I composed in one day Adamberger's aria in A, Cavalieri's in B-flat, and the trio, and copied them out in a day and a half." These are three pieces from *Die Entführung aus dem Serail,* numbering, not counting the recitatives, 371 measures of music. Another evidence of his great speed is the manuscript of the six German dances (K. 509), composed at Prague in 1787, which shows through the use of every possible time-saving device and abbreviation, the haste with which it was written. The oft repeated story is that Mozart had been invited by Count Pachta for dinner an hour before the other guests arrived, just enough time to compose the promised dance pieces!

If we may question that the fourteen-year-old boy was able to write down, after one hearing, Allegri's *Miserere* for nine voices, we cannot dismiss other feats, such as the one Mozart relates to his father in a letter of April 8, 1781. He writes: "Today (for I am writing at eleven o'clock at night) we had a concert, where three of my compositions were performed — new ones, of course: a rondo for a concerto for Brunetti; a sonata with violin accompaniment for myself, which I composed last night between eleven and twelve (but in order to be able to finish it, I only wrote out the accompaniment for Brunetti and retained my own part in my head); and then a rondo for Ceccarelli, which he had to repeat." The autograph of this sonata for piano and violin (K. 379), owned by the Library of Congress, bears out Mozart's statement: the violin part of the autograph is written in a light yellowish shade of ink from beginning to end; the piano part, however, is notated in short-

---

[2] See *The Letters of Mozart and His Family,* by Emily Anderson, London, 1938. I wish to acknowledge my gratitude to Miss Anderson for her kind permission to quote from her translation.

hand with the same shade of ink and later traced in dark ink, when
Mozart had the time to complete the piano score. Actually, the piano
part of the last variation with coda was entered on a new leaf after he
had crossed out the sketchy draft for it on the opposite page. The most
famous and extraordinary evidence of his prodigious mental capacity is
revealed in a letter to his sister, April 20, 1782, sending her the manuscript of a prelude and a three-part fugue (K. 394): "It is awkwardly
done, for the prelude ought to come first and the fugue to follow. But I
composed the fugue first and wrote it down while I was thinking out
the prelude."

From these and numerous similar stories we can surmise that
Mozart must have had a photographic memory and could compose
music faster than his pen would write. He must have worked out many
compositions in his head before he sat down to put them on paper. The
tale that he composed the overture to *Don Giovanni* the night before
the performance gains in credibility if we assume that the whole piece
was worked out in his mind beforehand. He copied the music from an
imaginary score which he knew by heart.

*   *
*

Mozart's musical manuscripts can be divided into three classes:
sketches, unfinished compositions or fragments, and final autographs.
Although we have only a limited number of sketches, the existing speci-
mens clearly show two types. The first one deals with melodic lines.
Many such sketches serve mainly as memoranda, hurriedly jotted-down
musical ideas for future use. These consist most frequently of a single
line without any indication of accompaniment, written on leaves that he
could carry around in his portfolio wherever he went. Sometimes they
amount to no more than a simple ditty, such as an eight-measure period
of a minuet, which makes one wonder why he bothered at all with the
reminder; sometimes he writes the first twenty measures of a movement
or a second theme for it, which he calls "Mittelgedanke." Considering
Mozart's conscientiousness about prosody, we are not surprised to find
extensive sketches for vocal compositions. The natural and beautiful line
of *Deh vieni non tardar,* from *Le Nozze di Figaro,* was not a spontaneous invention, but the result of several attempts. Although he
sketched the melody of the Terzetto for male voices *Del gran regno* (K.
434), he never bothered to finish the fair copy, which still exists in the

form of a fragment. It is a fortunate circumstance that we have a few sketches for both finales of *Die Zauberflöte;* they are, however, preliminary studies rather than complete drafts.

More numerous and more revealing are Mozart's sketches of the second type, which deal with passages of polyphonic texture. For the finale of the Piano Quartet in E-flat (K. 493), he jots down the main melody on one line, indicating violin and clavier with "V" and "Cl"; but when he changes to polyphonic texture, he uses three staves for violin, viola, and 'cello. That polyphonic writing requires more detailed work is self-evident. Mozart worked out on sketch leaves, which are still in existence, the three simultaneously played dance tunes in different meters for the ball-room scene of *Don Giovanni,* a challenging problem for any composer.

Particularly difficult for him was the composition of the canon *E nel tuo, nel mio bicchiero* from the finale to the second act of *Così fan tutte:* only after three attempts did Mozart arrive at the wonderful solution in the final version. Even the less complex canons, which he wrote for the entertainment of his friends, did not come to him easily. The legend that he tossed off a canon at the slightest provocation has little foundation in truth. By chance, we have his laborious sketches for some of these unassuming pieces. Since a few canons have come down to us with several texts, it is very likely that Mozart used old ones over again with new texts to suit the occasion — a practice common with other composers of the time.

The crucial question is: are we to infer from the small number of existing sketches that Mozart, as a rule, did not work out complete drafts for his compositions? Constanze's remark that she destroyed "the unusable autographs" of her husband (letter to André of July 21, 1800) would seem to indicate that she disposed of many sketches, because she offered even the unfinished compositions for sale to Breitkopf & Härtel, in her mistaken belief that any versatile composer could turn her husband's ingenious beginnings into finished works of pure gold. These "unusable autographs" may have contained the drafts for the big ensembles and the opera finales, which require more preparatory work. Mozart was capable of working out a composition in his imagination and then writing it down from memory. But for works of large proportions he undoubtedly made drafts beforehand, all of which evidently have been lost. It is a rule, with few exceptions, that composers discard the preliminary studies of a work after its completion.

Mozart left us more than a hundred fragments — unfinished compositions in which he lost interest, sometimes after he had written down as many as 120 measures. At other times he breaks off, for no reason we can see, after only ten or twenty measures, that is to say, after the first theme. A great many fragments are designed as opening movements, but some are attempts at a second movement or a finale, which Mozart simply crossed out. Occasionally he failed to do so, however, as in his Piano Trio in E major (K. 542), where he substituted a new piece for the 65-measure fragment. The substitution seems to be an improvement, although the original idea would have served adequately.

We can be reasonably sure that Mozart had no plan for the later use of the discarded beginnings of middle and last movements, but we are uncertain about his intentions concerning the beginnings of first movements. Some of them, if completed, might have become masterpieces. That he left them unfinished is baffling and cannot be explained by the assumption that the material would not have lent itself to further development. A few pieces may have remained torsos for the simple reason that Mozart lost interest in the medium. Sometimes he wrote down different beginnings of a work before settling upon the one he wished to carry to completion. The existence of these numerous fragments proves once again the overflow of his musical inventiveness. His wealth of melodic ideas, a manifestation of his creative exuberance, never seemed to diminish throughout his lifetime.

The state of these fragments permits another glimpse into Mozart's workshop. They often begin in full score with prepared staves for the individual instruments (and voices). In the first few measures, Mozart may write out all the parts, but then he continues to write down only the main melodic line, which he distributes among the various instruments, and the accompanying bass part; the other staves are left blank. He may go on for a while in this fashion, until he reaches a point at which a polyphonic passage necessitates the scoring of other parts. In works with voices Mozart writes out the vocal line and the instrumental bass, but includes the other instruments only in the ritornello or interlude section, or when one of them is used as a concertizing foil for the voice. It is obvious that the filling-in of the rest of the accompanying parts would have been a more mechanical job, and would constitute a secondary stage of his creative process.

There is nothing tentative about these fragments. In contrast to the sketches, which Mozart often wrote in a hardly legible script, sometimes as bad as Beethoven's, and with extensive use of his own brand of short-hand, the fragments are very neatly written. Many of them have specific indications for dynamics and expression marks, which, in itself, proves that they were not just memoranda, but that the composer intended to bring them to completion.

The most famous torsos, the most regrettable losses for us, are the Mass in C minor, of 1782, and the Requiem, his last work. Both were left unfinished for reasons well known. Mozart had promised the Mass as an offering to his bride, and its completion was no longer urgent after the wedding. His failure to complete this great work may also be due to the ban on concerted church music in Austria at about that time — a ban that was not lifted until 1790.

Mozart made extreme efforts to complete the Requiem and worked at it until death took his pen away. Had he received the commission ten years before, he would very likely have finished the work in six months (the time allotted to him in 1791), in spite of other commitments. But music of such emotional intensity could not be composed in a hurry. It was not his failing health and certainly not lack of inspiration that slowed him down, but the demands he placed upon himself during his last years with respect to complexity and depth of conception. While the Introit and the Kyrie are fully scored, for the Sequence and the Offertory he composed only all the voice parts and occasionally snatches for the instruments when the voices stopped or when he wanted to establish an important accompaniment figure. That he had to leave the Requiem unfinished must have filled him with great mental anguish. On the first page of the score we find Mozart's signature and the date 1792, assumed to be in his handwriting. This year Mozart never lived to see.

All the fragments seem to have one characteristic in common. Mozart starts out with the melody and bass line, and whether he stops to fill in other parts or not, the fragments end with the trailing-off of these two parts. The melody line need not be the top line of the score — which is, in Mozart's time, the violin (still the most important melodic vehicle) — but may be carried by an oboe, flute, or bassoon. This makes for the curious appearance of the page, with melodic bits strewn all over the otherwise blank score. When Mozart uses a polyphonic texture, he fills in the parts involved — a definitive indication that contrapuntal passages are planned from the outset and belong to his primary musical conception.

What can be observed in the fragments, the final scores corroborate. Of course, in completed works all the parts are filled in, and only a closer examination of the script yields clues to the creative process. The autographs and even the better facsimiles show the different hues of ink and the change in quill points. The ink colors vary from a light shade of yellowish brown to a deep black. The stems of notes can be extremely fine or thick, depending upon whether the quill has been freshly cut or worn. From the autographs we can discern that the music was written at different times. This again points to various stages of composition.

After a dozen measures or so, Mozart usually stops his melody and bass lines to fill in the accompanying parts; but sometimes he goes on indefinitely, as though to keep up with the flow of his inspiration, leaving the rest for a more leisurely time. Often too, one can observe that the melody line was written with great haste, and lacks the meticulous calligraphy of the other parts. When Mozart wants to nail down his musical ideas in a hurry, his dynamic signs, otherwise often beautifully written, are scribbled carelessly. But there is no consistency about this: in other instances, his melody line and bass are written with shapely and carefully formed notes, while the rest of the orchestration is rather fleetingly done. May we take this as an indication that whenever the melody line is written with great care, Mozart copied the music from a previous sketch? At any rate, there must have been a time-interval between his writing of the melody and of the subsidiary parts.

The orchestral parts that served purely as accompaniment were often not included in the score at all. The autograph of the G major symphony (K. 318) of 1779 has no space for the two trumpet parts, and therefore Mozart wrote them on separate leaves. For the same reason he left out all the wind instruments in scoring the big ensembles and the tutti finales of his operas. The manuscript paper that he used most often contained only twelve staves. Thus he was forced to write a separate score for the winds, which must have been worked out after the main score was finished. The wind instruments play, indeed, a subsidiary role in the tutti finales of *Le Nozze di Figaro, Don Giovanni, La Clemenza di Tito,* and *Die Zauberflöte.* In the letter to his father of July 20, 1782, he remarks specifically that "the Turkish music, trumpets, drums, flutes, and clarinets" could not be incorporated in the score of *Die Entführung,* because he could not get any music paper with sufficient lines. These instruments gave the score an exotic flavor, so popular with contemporary audiences. In the creative process they are, however, as unessential as the winds in all tuttis, to which they add only color and volume. The filling-in of inner lines is of an entirely different nature and represents an intrinsic part of Mozart's composing technique. It is the change in his conception of the music for the inner parts that was to bring about an important change in his musical creation.

In 1782, Mozart reached a crisis in his personal and artistic life, loosening himself from the fetters of both court life and parental domination. It was not only and not primarily the autocratic régime of Archbishop Colloredo that had smothered him and forced him to leave Salzburg, but rather his inner need to free himself from the overpowering influence of his father. He yearned for personal freedom and artistic independence, having long since outgrown the guiding hand of his father, who had only a vague conception of the spread of wings of which his son was capable. Mozart projected his resentment of this situation towards the Archbishop and forced this imperious potentate, by insubordination, to dismiss him. In a futile attempt to make his father understand, he explained in numerous letters that he could not sustain the insults to his honor.

Leopold had developed his son with loving care from a child prodigy to a mature musician, but in reality had fulfilled his own needs and, as time went on, tried to force Mozart into a position of emotional dependence upon him. The young Mozart idolized his father and tried to emulate him in every way; even his musical handwriting was the image of Leopold's. At the age of twenty-six he asked his father to write out the alphabet for him, in capital and small letters, so that he might continue to practice and improve his own hand. Only through the outward rebellion against the Archbishop was it possible for him to break loose from the strong domination of his father, whom he both loved and resented. Thus, he transferred his subconscious aversion for his father and cut himself loose from the hated atmosphere of Salzburg. Freedom once gained, feelings of guilt led him to manifest his filial devotion in his letters. He even went so far as to urge Leopold to quit his post in Salzburg and join him in Vienna, knowing full well that this was not feasible.

This new independence and his life in a broader cultural climate opened up new artistic perspectives and brought his creative genius to fruition. After he became acquainted with the recent symphonies and quartets of Joseph Haydn and with the works of Bach and Handel, in the circle of Baron van Swieten, he must have felt inadequate and in need of further studies. He copied for himself fugues and canons from the masters of the 17th and 18th centuries. We still possess his autograph copies of a fantasia by Froberger and a canon by Byrd. He studied the theorists from Fux to Kirnberger. In those years he wrote many fugues, most of them unfinished, and canons, which could have served only as exercises in the polyphonic idiom. It is hard to believe that in a letter to his sister, of April 20, 1782, he called the fugue "the most artistic and beautiful of all musical forms."

Of all the new music Vienna had to offer, it was Haydn's "Russian" String Quartets of 1781 that left the deepest imprint upon him. In these works, Haydn had achieved a true chamber-music style, in which four self-sustained instrumental parts are cast into a higher form of synthesis. Mozart's attempts in this style show the struggle he went through to achieve the perfection of the models. In his string quartets K. 387, 421, and 428 of 1782 and 1783, the music itself shows the labor of its creation. The autographs, with their numerous erasures and corrections, are even more revealing. He added three more quartets, K. 458, 464, 465, in the next two years, and these exhibit greater mastery of the new technique. When he dedicated all six of them to his friend Haydn, he wrote almost diffidently, "They are, indeed, the fruit of a long and laborious study; but the hope which my friends have given me that this toil will be in some degree rewarded, encourages me."

In contrast to the beautifully written manuscript of *Eine kleine Nachtmusik,* the autographs of the quartets of about the same period are by no means models of calligraphy. Most of the corrections are concerned with matters of detail. Only rarely does Mozart make any changes in the melodic line, which he upon occasion may transfer from one instrument to another, for instance from the first to the second violin, or from the 'cello to the viola. This is a new orientation in part-writing inspired by Haydn's models. In the *style galant* the inner parts had served as an accompaniment to fill in the harmony. Now these parts carry self-sustained melodic lines in the fashion of the obbligato accompaniment. They take on organic life and form integral parts of the composition, in contrast to the style of solo arias with concerted instruments — a style Mozart had mastered to perfection in his *Idomeneo* of 1780. Not only do the instrumental parts of his later quartets and other chamber works consist of self-sustained musical ideas, but they share the same thematic material. They constitute, so to speak, a homogeneous web of interrelated musical lines.

When Mozart wrote the scores of his late works, his creative process had not changed basically. He was still concerned with writing the melody line and bass first. In his earlier works the composition of inner parts had offered no problems: they simply filled in the harmony and therefore represent a reasonable facsimile of his mental image, conceived at the primary stage of his creative process. When in the later works his technique changed, the inner parts were not conceived immediately; they had to be worked out and molded into shape during the secondary stage of his creative process. His productivity decreased, not only for psychological reasons, but also on account of the complexity of his new style of writing. He could still dash off compositions with a simpler texture, such as innumerable minuets, German dances, and contra dances, in fulfillment of his duties as a chamber composer at the Imperial Court, although they too profited from his growing skill and refinement in part-writing. Most other compositions required greater concentration and toil. In their numerous vital corrections and extensive alterations, the autograph scores of *Le Nozze di Figaro* and *Don Giovanni* show his difficulty with the new musical idiom.

In some instances we have proof that Mozart worked out on separate sheets of paper any passage that involved intricate part-writing or polyphonic devices. Unfortunately, we have no sketches for the fugato passages of the famous finale to the *Jupiter Symphony*. In spite of its effectiveness, the music reveals some traces of the labor pains of its creator. While this movement was fully worked out before Mozart entered it in the score, and therefore the manuscript shows little of his creative process, there is an interesting change in the coda of the slow movement which, in its original form, did not include the return of the first theme. Musical afterthoughts of this nature can be found in a number of works.

At the time Mozart composed *Die Zauberflöte,* he wrote to his wife in Baden, on July 2, 1791, and asked her to tell Süssmayr "to send me my score of the first act, from the introduction to the finale, so that I may orchestrate it." On the next day he wrote: "I trust that Süssmayr will not forget to copy out at once what I left for him: and I am counting on receiving today those portions of my score for which I asked." It would seem that Mozart had finished the first act in the form of a draft with complete melodic lines, which Süssmayr was to have copied out, probably for the singers.

The different stages of composition can also be observed in the score of the Requiem. If we can assume that the complex polyphony of the Introit and the Kyrie must have been worked out beforehand on sketch leaves from which the music was copied in the autograph, the accompanying orchestral parts were composed later. At the very beginning the main musical lines are written in larger notes for basset horns and bassoons, and the syncopated staccato accompaniment of the strings has smaller notes in a different shade of ink. Even though they are in all probability a musical afterthought, these suffocated sighs of the violins give the movement a dirge-like character and enhance the atmosphere of sadness and resignation.

* *
*

From the sketch material still in existence, from the condition of the fragments, and from the autographs themselves we can draw definite conclusions about Mozart's creative process. To invent musical ideas he did not need any stimulation; they came to his mind "ready-made" and in polished form. In contrast to Beethoven, who made numerous attempts at shaping his musical ideas until he found the definitive formulation of a theme, Mozart's first inspiration has the stamp of finality. Any Mozart theme has completeness and unity: as a phenomenon it is a *Gestalt*. Beethoven's themes achieve this quality only through an elaborate process of metamorphosis.

In Mozart's primary stage of conception, whether he works out a composition in his mind or on paper, melody line and bass are safely established, while the accompanying middle parts remain undefined. In his earlier works the writing of inner parts offers no difficulty, since these parts function merely as harmonic support: this under-pinning was created simultaneously with the melodic idea. In his later works, however, the composition of these inner parts, whose musical lines contain organic life of their own, forms a secondary stage of his creation.

Before Mozart wrote down the fair copy of a composition it had been worked out mentally in the form of an imaginary sketch from which he copied the music, as it were, from memory. For works of large proportions he made stenographic drafts consisting of melody and bass, while the orchestration and details were left for a more leisurely time. Music of polyphonic texture was a problem. Since contrapuntal writing did not come to him easily, he prepared it on separate sketch leaves before entering it in his score. The passages of double counterpoint and in fugal or canon style are so skilfully and unobtrusively woven into the fabric of the music that a listener is hardly aware of the beautiful craftsmanship. It is the balance and integration of all component parts that make for his real greatness.

Mozart's contemporaries had little conception of his genius, and therefore the world treated him with neglect and, at times, with scorn. He was, as we know, no revolutionary; he spoke the musical language of his time. He made liberal use of musical ideas of others, the urge for originality being as alien to him as to any composer of his time. The creeds of the Enlightenment are reflected in his formal designs, which never overstep conventional boundaries, and his graceful and charming melodies are late flowers of the *style galant*. Throughout his life Mozart adhered to the esthetic doctrines of Rococo art. He expressed this eloquently in the well-known letter to his father of September 26, 1781: "Passions, whether violent or not, must never be expressed in such a way as to excite disgust; and music, even in the most terrible situations, must never offend the ear, but must please the hearer, or in other words, must never cease to be music."

The prolific output of a man who died at the age of thirty-five was nothing unusual at that time; neither was the speed with which he could turn out his works. Composers like Leopold Gassmann, Paul Wranitzky, Wenzel Müller, Albrechtsberger, and Salieri could write music just as fast — music that was, for the audience at large, just as pleasant to listen to as any of Mozart's. His music could and still can be perceived on two levels. He was quite aware that the charm of the music would speak to the uninitiated audience, and that, at the same time, its sophistication would delight the discriminating ears of the connoisseurs. In a letter to his father, of December 28, 1782, he writes: "There are passages here and there from which connoisseurs alone can derive satisfaction, but these passages are written in such a way that the less learned cannot fail to be pleased, though without knowing why." The attentive and knowledgeable listener and student of his music will discover at each performance new enchanting details, while the untutored ear responds to the clarity and directness of his musical language. Still, there is no conceptual dichotomy noticeable. Whatever he writes, whether it is a work commissioned by a wealthy patron or a piece for the entertainment of his friends, or for his own satisfaction, without any particular performance purpose in mind, his music speaks with finality of expression.

What the majority of contemporary listeners found in Mozart, they could have found in a great many other composers. The profound depth of his music, the intensity of its emotional content, as well as its wonderful craftsmanship, had to escape an audience whose ears could not perceive anything beyond the sensuous sound, the beauty of melody and harmony. His real greatness was hidden behind a curtain they could not lift. Neither the pleasure-loving aristocracy nor the bourgeoisie could grasp the innuendos of this music, the fine characterization, the in-between shades of moods, the dualistic juxtaposition of reality and illusion in his operas. The enthusiastic reception of *Die Zauberflöte* in Vienna rested not upon the wonderful music or an understanding of its profound symbolism and its high ethical concepts but rather upon the enjoyment of the fairy-tale, the theatrical tricks, the supernatural elements, and the surprises. The combination of light comedy and of the most moving and deeply felt music Mozart ever wrote lifts *Così fan tutte* to a plane of sublime humor that even later generations did not comprehend.

His wife and most of his personal friends had no conception of his greatness. His wealthy patron, Baron van Swieten, a connoisseur of the arts and letters, was so short-sighted as to advise Mozart's widow to order a third-class funeral, for he was apparently not willing to advance the money for a more dignified service. Thus, Mozart was buried in a pauper's grave, all traces of which disappeared completely. Even his death mask, which Constanze had preserved for a number of years, eventually broke into pieces. But Mozart, thanks to the foresight of Johann Anton André, left us something that shows better what the man was like than any representation could convey — his musical manuscripts. Those discolored and often frayed leaves contain the music that fills us with delight and that represents a more eloquent monument to his genius than any marble tombstone.

# ON MOZART'S RHYTHM

## By EDWARD E. LOWINSKY

Humbly dedicated to Mozart's memory and written for one of his greatest admirers, Erwin Panofsky: humanist, art historian, and Mozart connoisseur extraordinary.

WHEN Mozart encountered Bach's music for the first time in his life at Baron van Swieten's, he wrote, under the impact of this event, a fugue in C major (K. 394, 1782). It shows a marvelous command of fugal technique with its tonal answer, its modulation plan, its episodes, its strettos, augmentations, and diminutions. What a paradox this fugue presents: it has all of Bach's technique and none of his style! The reason for this paradox is that there are features of musical expression that lie so deep below the surface of musical consciousness that the composer, remaining unaware of them, cannot change them. Rhythm, meter, phrase structure — these are elements as natural, and

Ex. 1 Fugue in C major for piano, K. 394
Andante maestoso

31

therefore ordinarily as withdrawn from consciousness, as are breathing, speaking, and walking.

The frequent shift of meter and accent, the natural irregularity of phrasing in a Bach fugue are replaced in Mozart's fugue by a regularity of metrical design and a periodicity of phrasing that are utterly un-Bachian (see Ex. 1).

The subject is two measures long, it enters at intervals of two measures; the stress is placed on one and three in each measure, it is inherent in the melodic outline and reinforced by a counterpoint that is ostensibly independent but actually closely modelled in phrasing and accent after the fugue subject itself. Dissonances on the first and third beat (mm. 4 and 6) add to the feeling of stress. Nothing of the subtle polyrhythmic and polymetric design that are essential elements in the continuity and flow of Bach's music. Periodicity, symmetry of phrase structure, regular recurrence of stress are so much part of Mozart's musical thinking that it is superfluous to illustrate them. Wherever we open his scores we find them present in every movement, almost in every theme. But Mozart was entirely too sensitive not soon to detect the artistic value of Bach's freedom in stress and phrase, and too much of a craftsman not to experiment with it. In the same year 1782, only a few months after he wrote the fugue, Mozart composed a serenade in C minor for eight wind instruments (K. 388) which he later arranged as a string quintet (K. 406). The first movement shows a pattern unusual for Mozart in its irregularity of phrase groupings and use of uneven numbers. The first theme section and bridge are grouped in nine, three, four, six, six, six, and seven measures, the second theme and epilogue in six, six, six, seven, eight, eight, four, four, four, four. In each case the seven measures are an extension of a six-measure unit, in the first theme section the extension occurs before the entry of the second theme, the second time it occurs in the last phrase rounding out the second theme. Similar extensions, e.g. of four- to five-measure phrases, especially before the entrance of the second theme, can be found also in other works of Mozart. Aside from the seven-measure phrases there is definite proportion in the seeming disorder and a clear tendency to return to symmetric regularity after an irregular beginning.

A rather unique case of studied irregularity presents itself in Mozart's last string quartet, in F (K. 590). The first movement starts out with a theme of three measures. The irregularity of this theme is heightened by the stress on measure 2 emphasized by a *forte* in contrast to the *piano*

Ex. 2 String Quartet in F major, K. 590, 1st movement

Allegro moderato

of measure 1 and by the curious breaking off on an unaccented beat
after an impetuous run. But the symmetrical answer shows that inner
force operating in Mozart's mind that immediately restores the disturbed equilibrium. On the other hand, his refusal to give the same
stress to the second measure of the consequent (m. 5) as to that of the
antecedent (m. 2) by expressing the second phrase *piano* throughout,
introduces an element of dynamic asymmetry and shows a delicacy in the
treatment of stress lacking entirely, for instance, in Johann Christian
Bach's phrasing (see Ex. 8). The three-measure phrase is felt throughout
the movement, but it is balanced by the clear phrase structure of the
second theme divided into two phrases of four measures each.

The Minuet of the same quartet is dominated by the number seven.
The first part consists of two phrases each of seven measures:

Ex. 3 String Quartet in F major, K. 590, 3rd movement, Menuetto

Allegretto

The second part consists of twice fourteen measures. The Trio of the Minuet takes the uneven number five left out thus far. Its first part consists of two five-measure phrases:

Ex. 4 String Quartet in F major, K.590, 3rd movement, Trio

The second part begins with an eight-measure phrase and continues with three five-measure phrases.

Two conclusions seem obvious: if Mozart's phrases are irregular, they are so by design. But even his irregularity is regular. He cannot escape his inner law. The genuine and spontaneous irregularity of phrase

Ex. 5 Haydn, Piano Sonata in A-flat major, 1st movement

structure that one often encounters in Haydn is foreign to Mozart. The beginning of Haydn's Piano Sonata in A-flat major (Ex. 5), patterned in phrases of three, two and one-half, two and one-half, four, five, offers an example of freely changing phrases that would be hard to find in Mozart. An external symbol of Mozart's desire for lucidity is the use of pauses not only for purposes of articulation, but also to clarify and to delimit a phrase. The first theme of the Piano Sonata in D (K. 311), composed at Mannheim in 1777, is characteristic, especially if compared with Haydn:

Ex. 6 Piano Sonata, D major, K. 311, 1st movement

Clarity and lucidity—manifest also in the transparent texture, the concise formal structure, the preference for the middle registers — are only one side of Mozart's genius. They cannot account for the immense vitality of his art. What is it that gives a Mozartean theme that inimitable verve, that quality which sets it apart from Dittersdorf or Johann Christian Bach as much as from Stamitz and Haydn?

Let us observe a typical Mozart theme, from the Piano Sonata in B-flat (K. 333):

Ex. 7 Piano Sonata in B-flat major, K. 333, 1st movement

The metrical stresses, although seemingly regular, are in reality of a very subtle and almost elusive quality. In the first four measures the stress on one is followed by a lighter stress on the dotted second quarter; the elasticity and lightness achieved in this way are enhanced by the accompaniment, which avoids a stress on one and two by starting on the time interval between them; in measure 5 the stresses on one and three are stronger by virtue of their character as appoggiaturas; in measure 7 the appoggiatura stress falls on each one of the four quarters.

Rhythmically, we observe a great diversity of motion arranged in patterns of free symmetry: measures 3 and 4 correspond to 1 and 2, but not literally; measures 7 and 8 correspond to 5 and 6, but the difference is even stronger here, and measures 9 and 10, which round off the whole theme, are connected with the preceding phrase but not paired off as the first two groups are. Symmetry and variation, order and freedom, similarity and difference are joined in a highly sophisticated pattern.

The rate of change and variation are by no means subject to chance. From beginning to end the theme unfolds with steadily increasing motion. To appreciate fully the art that reigns here, it is useful to compare Mozart's theme with a similar theme by Johann Christian Bach, the opening of Opus V, No. 3:

**Ex. 8**   Joh. Chr. Bach, Piano Sonata in G major, Op. V, No. 3, 1st movement

It would be difficult to find in 18th-century music a theme at once so Mozartean in its initial inspiration and so utterly un-Mozartean in its elaboration. Instead of variation of stress we find a uniformly heavy stress on one reinforced by the accompaniment stressing one and three in regular sequence and scarcely relieved by the very light stress on two in measures 1, 3, 5, 6; instead of the light treatment of the appoggiatura in measure 2 we find it here underscored by the rhythm 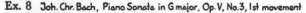 ; instead

of free symmetry we have here mechanical symmetry (mm. 1-2 = 3-4);
instead of motivic variation and evolution (Ex. 7, mm. 5-8) we find
here the initial motif literally chased to death (Ex. 8, mm. 5-6); instead
of a gradually increasing motion engendering increased interest, we have
uniform motion which, paired as it is with motivic repetition and duplication of the harmonic pattern (mm. 1-4: I-IV-V-I; mm. 5-8:
I-IV-I $^6_4$ V-I), reduces the listener's interest to the point of tedium. The
effect of the slight rhythmic variation in measure 7 is immediately can-
celled by literal repetition and ruined by the clumsy ending, which uses
for the fifth time in eight measures the rhythmic pattern ♩♩♩♩ ♩ — a
passage that Mozart might have saved by accelerated motion and by
gliding into the ending, possibly in this manner:

Ex. 9

To round out the picture of Johann Christian Bach's composing method
we add a few more observations: measures 9-12 continue with a
restatement of measures 1-4, except that measures 11-12 modulate to
D major; the development section starts with a literal restatement of the
first theme (mm. 1-8) in the dominant; the same theme is dragged
through eleven further measures; the place of the second theme is taken
by a running passage of sixteenths devoid of character and suffering
even from mechanical duplication — literal sequence has here dulled
to literal repetition; the second theme section consisting of sixteen measures appears at the end of the sonata in exact repetition transposed
from dominant to tonic. Yet, compared to some of his contemporaries,
Johann Christian Bach appears subtle. Ditters von Dittersdorf opens his
String Quartet No. 6 in A major with an eight-measure theme (Ex. 10).
Here the original idea is just one measure long. Whatever it may have
of freshness or grace is ruined by excessive repetition and complete lack
of variation. The two main motifs *a* and *b* appear three times, *a* in the
form of an unrelieved sequence, *b* in literal repetition. The same monotony dominates the metrical picture: the stress on one reigns un-
mitigated and without the slightest variation. If we add to this the fact
that motif *a* reappears 27 times, motif *b* 15 times in the further course

Ex. 10  D. von Dittersdorf, String Quartet in A major, No. 6, 1st movement

of the movement we may be able to gauge the devastating effect that this mechanical repetition of material not too interesting to begin with must produce. To prove that it is not the initial idea but the manner of its elaboration that distinguishes Mozart from Johann Christian Bach or Dittersdorf, let us observe how his theme would suffer from a similar procedure:

Ex. 11

But there is no need to bowdlerize Mozart. For the composer himself gave a perfectly clear illustration of this kind of composing in his immortal joke, *Ein musikalischer Spass,* the horn sextet in F major (K. 522). In the first theme of the opening movement he parodies a com-

Ex. 12  Horn Sextet in F major, K. 522, 1st movement, 2 horns

poser unable to construct a phrase properly: the antecedent goes

the same way as the consequent, the consequent is consequently no consequent, the antecedent no antecedent, the ending the same as the beginning. And what monotony and heaviness of stress and of rhythm!
Add to this the rhythmic scheme of the opening theme of the fourth
movement — and nothing more need be said.

Ex. 13  Horn Sextet in F major, K. 522, last movement, Violin I

The comparison between Johann Christian Bach and Dittersdorf on
the one hand and Mozart on the other reveals a fundamental difference:
the minor composer spends his invention in the first few measures, the
rest is more or less self-perpetuating; the theme takes care of itself
through established techniques of elaboration. A minimum of invention
is used with a maximum of repetition. The great composer never abdi-
cates in favor of automatic propagation. He works as hard at the continuation, the climax, and the end of a phrase or a whole composition
as at the beginning, indeed, even more so. No break between invention
and elaboration mars his work, he is permanently engaged with all his
powers of concentration and imagination.

*   *<br>*

Mozart's rhythmic genius was by no means a gift laid in the cradle
by a smiling Muse. It suffices to quote one theme from a work written
in the summer of 1773, the Serenade in D (K. 185):

Ex. 14  Serenade No. 3, K. 185, third movement, Violino solo

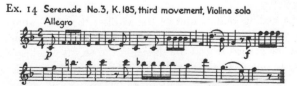

The same Mozart who in 1773 composed a theme that had not yet reached the level of a Johann Christian Bach or even a Dittersdorf wrote in 1778 the B-flat-major sonata for piano (Ex. 7) and in 1785 the D-minor Piano Concerto in which the solo part begins with a theme that has no match in music literature for the marvelous fusion of a deeply moving *espressivo* with rhythmic vitality.

Ex. 15 Piano Concerto, D minor, K. 466, 1st movement, piano solo, m. 77-91

Although the character of this theme is entirely different from that of the B-flat-major theme, we observe here as there diversity of motion, subtle variation of primary and secondary stresses, arrangement in freely symmetrical patterns which are never quite alike, gradual increase in motion, and that gain of momentum near the end that seems to summon all rhythmic and metric forces at precisely the point where usually relaxation of tension prevails. *And metric forces*: for the accumulation of stresses near the end, due to melodic figuration as well as to harmonic change and observable in Example 7 also, has an effect similar to the increase in motion.

It is the ending that manifests the virility, the classical temper of Mozart's genius. Many a Romantic composer would have found it hard to resist the temptation to end the theme in the way it was begun, thereby reducing feeling to sentimentality and robbing the theme of its soaring climax:

Ex. 16

The increase in motion also affects the phrase structure. The theme begins with a pair of symmetrical two-measure phrases, it ties the following two phrases into one four-measure unit by means of syncopation and harmonic tension, and it ends surprisingly with a seven-measure unit. The fourth measure of the final phrase presents an elision: it is at once the last measure of the preceding and the first of the following phrase. Mozart contracts two four-measure phrases by elision into one continuous seven-measure phrase. We see here again pauses used not only for articulation, but also to clarify phrase structure: two measures, pause — two measures, pause — four measures, pause — seven measures, pause. Increased motion goes hand in hand with accumulation of stresses and growing length of phrases.

The asymmetry growing out of a perfectly symmetrical conception is due to the continuous increase in motion. It is an asymmetry so deeply imbedded in symmetry that it is always felt as a charming deviation caused by an overflow of vitality. We observe precisely the same phenomenon in two beautifully shaped themes of 13 and 11 measures respectively of the Finale from the same Concerto, which we quote to enable the reader to study in convenient juxtaposition a few of the infinite variations with which Mozart realizes his rhythmic principle. The first of these themes is shown in Ex. 17. Had Mozart used the technique of mechanical symmetry which was the vogue of the period, his theme would have had the shape shown in Ex. 18. The heavy stress on one would have been unrelieved by that stress on two — a favorite metrical device of Mozart's — which we now have in measures 8 and 11. Nor would we have known that exhilarating acceleration of measures 9 and 10 or the pleasant shock at being thrown out of the expected

Ex. 17 Piano Concerto in D minor, K.466, last movement, piano solo

Allegro assai

Ex. 18

regularity of phrase construction by the extra measure 10 responsible for the extension of twelve to thirteen measures.

And finally a word about that wonderful theme stretching over eleven measures (two and two and two and five, whereby five consists of a contraction of two and four) used by Mozart as a connecting link within the Rondo. This time we will give the mechanical solution first, Mozart's version second:

Ex. 19

Compare these twelve measures with Mozart's eleven-measure version:

Ex. 20 Piano Concerto in D minor, K. 466, last movement, piano solo

In Example 19 we have left the first eight measures untouched to show more clearly how decisive the acceleration in measure 8 and the resulting contraction and asymmetry are for the final effect of the theme. The strict symmetry of measures 9-12 in example 19 sounds lamely repetitious and arrests progress precisely at the expected high point of the phrase. Yet, Mozart's version reveals that the return of the first motif transposed to G minor was clearly in the composer's mind. For can we not see the motif D-F♯-G distributed over both hands in measures 8-9? Instead of pausing for three quarters and beginning the motif on the first beat of measure 9 in literal repetition, Mozart pauses for a mere dotted eighth and brings the motif in rhythmic contraction and metric change following through with the longest chain of eighth notes used so far in the theme. Again Mozart reserves his greatest surprise for the climax of the phrase and lets go with a maximum of rhythmic force as he nears the end.

The relationship between this theme and the first theme from the opening movement should not be overlooked. They stand next to each other like two portraits of one man showing him first in the flower of youth with all the fire and feeling of the adolescent and then as a man self-possessed, purposeful, and no longer carrying his emotions in mien and gesture for everyone to read. The emotional upbeat lifting the melody one octave higher has disappeared, so have the expressive appoggiaturas at the end of the phrase and the rhetorical interjections of the accompaniment. The theme appears reduced to its most essential form.

\*     \*

\*

The principle of increasing animation is, I believe, in one form or another present in almost all of Mozart's mature compositions. Acceleration may appear not only in increase of speed but in the lengthening of phrases: the progress from small to larger phrase units will create an impression of greater continuity (see the Minuet in Ex. 3, where the two seven-measure phrases are divided into units of three and four and two and five measures and where acceleration occurs not only within each phrase but also from phrase to phrase). The principle may appear in the sequence of themes, and in their elaboration: in many compositions increasing motion will be found in the first section of a sonata-allegro form up to the moment when the second theme appears, at which point a new wave of gradually increasing motion starts; indeed, the Mozartean trill that occurs so often at the conclusion of the first theme section or at the end of the recapitulation before the entrance of the coda and that extends over a whole measure is the natural consequence of the principle of acceleration: it is simply the high point of rhythmic vitality and must be played like that. Acceleration may manifest itself in polyphonic devices such as the use of strettos in phrases introduced before without stretto—the first movement of the C-major String Quintet (K. 515) offers beautiful illustrations of this procedure: rare are the works in which it does not manifest itself at all. Metric variation, too, will be found to be almost always present within the works of the mature Mozart (again the Minuet in Ex. 3 offers an illuminating illustration of accumulation of stress in mm. 4, 10, 11, 12, 13, and of change of stress through syncopation in m. 5, through metric change of the viola motif in m. 12).

The situation is different with respect to asymmetry. The law of symmetric correspondence is part and parcel of the Rococo style, which was Mozart's heritage; it is an irremovable element of his own mode of thinking. Even where we found asymmetry, it was only as a modification of symmetry. But though Mozart does use strict symmetry, it differs from that of a Johann Christian Bach or a Dittersdorf, and radically so. At times he creates symmetrical correspondence between small phrases of one or two measures, but he prefers, and especially in his later works, longer and more interesting phrases to begin with. A case in point is the String Quartet in A (K. 464), composed in 1785 and known as No. 5 of the six quartets dedicated to Haydn.

To demonstrate the fusion of Mozart's two principles of symmetry and increasing animation which both shape not only a phrase but a whole section we must quote the whole exposition:

Ex. 21

None of the six quartets opens with a theme more regular than does the one quoted here. Yet, even here we find a theme of sixteen measures, not divided into two pairs of four-four phrases, but in a pattern of four-four, two-two, and an unmatched final phrase of four. If the principle of symmetry dominates measures 1-8, that of increased motion takes possession of measures 9-16. Both principles are perfectly fused in measures 17-36. The polyphonic elaboration of the opening motif creates a continuum of eight measures, the largest we have had thus far, but the entries of the voices are spaced in perfect proportion in regular intervals of two measures. The C-major motif connecting the first and the second themes with each other (mm. 25ff.) is a fine demonstration of motivic contraction as a consequence of the high point of motion reached before the entrance of the second theme: a two-measure motif is contracted to a one-measure and finally to a one-quarter motif: the principle of increased motion is responsible for motivic contraction.

In the second theme section (in the dominant) the principle of increased motion works in two ways: not only is it responsible for the acceleration within this section, we observe furthermore greater animation in comparison with the preceding section. The triplet movement constitutes a speed-up compared with the eighth motion of the beginning and in measures 47-53 we have a continuous triplet motion accompanied by an accumulation of stresses — Mozart's favorite stress on two joining that on one. While the triplets give way to eighths from measure 54 on, another form of speed-up is effected by the use of a two-quarter motif which gives the appearance of a change from 3/4 to 2/4. The four measures of the 2/4 motif (mm. 54-57) are rounded out by a cadential phrase (mm. 58-61) the main motif of which appears in successively shortened and contracted form in the last acceleration before the entrance of the coda. But even within the coda we have another speed-up, which reaches its peak at mm. 79-82. The perfectly symmetrical last phrase of four measures with its clear articulation of the two halves allows us finally to catch our breath and relax.

The development section, too, is organized in successive waves of increased rhythmic intensity followed by a receding wave that smoothes the waters for a return of the beginning.

Another form of strict symmetry may be illustrated by the beginning of the Finale of the G-minor Symphony (K. 550). Equally clear examples of the same point are provided by the first eight measures of the

G-minor Piano Quartet (K. 478) and of the C-minor Piano Sonata (K. 457).

Ex. 22 Symphony in G minor, K. 550, last movement, Violin I

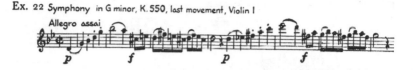

Here strict symmetry is called upon to provide the balance for the impetus generated by the conflict of two strongly contrasting motifs within one theme. The sequence of motifs is in each case determined by the principle of accelerated motion.

\* \*

\*

From our choice of illustrations it may appear as though the principle of increasing animation operated only in the fast movements of Mozart's works. The Andante in B-flat from the F-major Piano Sonata (K. 533), composed in 1788, one of the most beautiful slow movements written by Mozart, may demonstrate that this is by no means the case. Again, the principle of acceleration is responsible for the rhythmic shape of every phrase, for the rhythmic sequence of themes, for the changing length of phrases, and for the shape of the whole (see Ex. 23). The first speed-up occurs in measure 3 followed by a slight let-up in measure 4. In the next measures we see a continuous building up of steady motion: a phrase of eighth notes extending over almost two measures flows into a phrase extending over three full measures. The rhythmic intensification goes hand in hand with an increase in harmonic tension, accumulation of dissonance, and lengthening of phrases from four to six measures. In the ensuing repetition only the first eight measures are literally re-stated. Instead of the declining motion of measures 9-10 the corresponding measures of the repeated theme increase the motion by introducing sixteenth notes and extend the phrase from ten to twelve measures. As a further means of increasing tension, i.e. inner motion, Mozart, in a manner rarely found in his early work, leaves the theme open. Usually, if he leads a theme to the dominant, he guides it back to the tonic and then constructs a bridge leading to the second theme section in the dominant. Here repeated theme and bridge are amalgamated. Indeed, not anywhere in the whole movement, not even in the recapitulation, is the theme rounded off by a close in the tonic.

Ex. 23  Piano Sonata in B-flat major, K.333; 2nd movement

The initial motif of the first theme appears now in disguise as the second theme in the left hand, while the right hand increases the motion by a full measure of sixteenths. The syncopations of the ensuing measures apply the brake. The same happens in the next two measures, but a degree higher with increased tension. Then the sixteenth motion breaks through and flows unrestricted through the next five measures to a cadence on the dominant. Again increase in motion is matched by increase in phrase length, harmonic tension, dissonance, and growing deviation from the tonal center.

The third section, the coda, shows not only the same curve within itself, but also the further increase of motion by the organic addition of still smaller note values: sixteenth sextolets and thirty-seconds. The coda begins restfully enough with a phrase of two measures alternating in typical coda fashion between dominant and tonic — with F as the new tonic — and underscoring the feeling of being at home by basing the harmonic progression on the pedal point of the new tonic. But this feeling of calm merely precedes the high pitch of rhythmic and harmonic intensity. For the first phrase of two measures is now answered by the longest phrase of the exposition in a continuous motion over eleven measures. The rhythmic climax of the exposition is also the high point of harmonic tension: the deviation to F minor and A-flat major, the return to F minor by way of the Neapolitan sixth, the ensuing clearing up of F minor to F major through a chromatic bass line, the renewed deviation to D minor and final confirmation of F major — these constitute the most dramatic harmonic events of the exposition. Together with the rhythmic happenings they give the coda an inner tension and urgency for which we would seek in vain in a coda of Mozart's early works.

A result of the steady increase in motion throughout the exposition is the rather unusual pattern of phrase groupings:

```
      10                12                11                13
   ┌ 4 - 6 ┐         ┌ 4 - 8 ┐         ┌ 4 - 7 ┐         ┌ 2 - 11 ┐
    └ a                 a' ┘           └ b b' ┘           └ c - c' ┘
              A                         B                 C
             22                        11                13
```

Each consequent phrase within each group exceeds the preceding one while the phrase groupings grow in length so that two phrases of 10:12 are matched by two of 11:13, again a rather unusual grouping for Mozart.

But with the instinct of a sleepwalker Mozart restores the balance by matching asymmetrical phrases in a symmetrical manner. The development section is shaped in two groups of 13 measures. The recapitulation replaces the proportion 10:12 by 10:8 and the proportion 11:13 by 11:21, thus reserving the greatest extension and animation for the close of the movement.

\*     \*

\*

Mozart's rhythm is peculiarly his own. This becomes clear when we study the work of his greatest contemporary, Haydn. We choose a characteristic theme from Haydn's piano sonata composed in 1773, i.e. before Mozart exercised any influence on his style:

Ex. 24 Haydn, Piano Sonata in C major, 1st movement

This theme speaks with vigorous and rather regular stress and a nearly uniform rhythm of dotted thirty-seconds and quarter appoggiaturas which extends not only over the first theme, but over the bridge right into the second theme. What is true of Haydn's thematic work is true of his rhythmic organization: he loves to exploit one rhythmic as well as one motivic figure. What there is of increase in motion is due to a longer phrase or to an avoidance of stops rather than to genuine acceleration. Haydn's rhythm is impulsive: it moves in sudden spurts and stops, it loves surprise and shock and abrupt change. Whereas Mozart strives for gradual change and goes from one motion to the next degree of speed, Haydn likes to change from quarter to sixteenth or from eighth to thirty-second motion, if not even from quarters to thirty-seconds. The

Ex. 25 Haydn, Piano Sonata in G minor, 1st movement

Piano Sonata in G minor published in 1785, but composed before that time, shows well these qualities which Haydn learned to love in the works of Carl Philipp Emanuel Bach. (See Ex. 25.) Undoubtedly, the tendency towards continuous movement found in both composers is a legacy from Baroque style, in which both are rooted, while the love of strong contrast is a manifestation of the new style and its desire to overcome the uniformity of Baroque movement by spontaneity and sudden change. Yet, both elements are often found side by side.

Even though Mozart had a great influence on Haydn's later work, an influence that extends to rhythm and phrase structure, the characteristic vigor and impulsiveness of Haydn's rhythm can always be felt. A case in point is the great Sonata in E-flat major composed for Frau von Genzinger in 1789/90.

Ex. 26 Haydn, Piano Sonata in E-flat major, 1st movement

Allegro

The theme of the opening movement starts with a typical rhythmic gesture, forceful and abrupt and answered in a calmer but energetic manner; both phrases are repeated in a free sequence which is followed by a sudden outburst of sixteenths extending over slightly more than one measure, while it takes the theme three measures to come to a halt. The popular inspiration of this theme is easily seen if we present it stripped of ornamentation, in its essential outline revealing the large intervals and the harmonic character of an Austrian *Jodler*:

Ex. 27

Undoubtedly, the accentuation of Haydn's themes owes much of its vigor to popular song and dance.

The difference in character between Mozart and Haydn is reflected in the contrast of their rhythmic organization. It is a case of diversity versus unity, of growing animation versus consistency of motion, of gradual versus abrupt change, of sublime grace versus earthly vigor, of light and varied stress versus robust and regular accentuation, of a highly refined and personal stylization versus popular inspiration. Whether or not Haydn composed themes with increased rhythmic motion — and undoubtedly he did — the nature of that motion differs greatly and fundamentally from that of Mozart's.

*     *

*

We are not unmindful that we have left out of consideration the Mannheim symphonic style. A comparison might reveal that the new dynamism of that style remains a rather external, if certainly exciting, device, whereas Mozart's law of growing animation is a deep-seated principle pervading the musical structure in all of its aspects. The significance, variability, and evolution of this principle cannot, of course, be exhaustively treated in a brief essay. Indeed, we have not even touched upon Mozart's operas. Certainly, the principle of steadily increasing animation must apply to a dramatic form that is crowned by a rousing finale into which librettist and composer throw their combined resources. Yet, who is to say whether the principle was extended by Mozart to the field of opera, or whether it did not have its very origin in the dramatic instinct of an operatic genius?

# MOZARTEAN MODULATIONS[1]

## By HANS T. DAVID

IF it ever occurred to Mozart to look up the term *Modulation* in a German musical dictionary, he was bound to be disappointed. The only such work available, Johann Gottfried Walther's *Musicalisches Lexicon,*[2] had been published in the year Joseph Haydn was born. And Walther's definition for *modulatio* was "die Führung einer Melodie oder Sang-Weise; d. i. die Art und Weise, oder die Manier, womit ein Sänger oder Instrumentist die Melodie herausbringet" ("the inflection of a melody or line of song; that is, the manner and method, or the fashion, with which a singer or instrumentalist brings out the melody").

Walther, in his narrow and somewhat old-fashioned wording, did not follow the model of Sébastien de Brossard's *Dictionnaire de Musique,* which had been published a generation earlier.[3] Brossard distinguished between the meaning of the word in ancient and in modern usage. He indicated that modulation meant to his contemporaries not only the proper melodic treatment of a mode, but also "the regular progression of several parts, through the sounds that are in the harmony of any

[1] A paper read at the annual meeting of the American Musicological Society at Princeton University on Dec. 30, 1955, and slightly enlarged for publication. References to specific works have been concentrated on a few easily available compositions, primarily the Fantasy in C minor, K. 475; the String Quartet in G major, K. 387; and the Symphony in G minor, K. 550. The reader who would like to verify the majority of the analytical comments will also need a copy of the Piano Sonatas and a score of the String Quintet in G minor, K. 516; the Symphonies in D major, K. 385 ("Haffner") and K. 504 ("Prague"), E-flat major, K. 543, and C major, K. 551 ("Jupiter"); and *Ein musikalischer Spass,* K. 522.

[2] Leipzig, 1732. A facsimile reprint, edited by Richard Schaal, has appeared in *Documenta musicologica,* Kassel, 1953.

[3] Paris, 1703 and 1705. The book is mostly known in the *Troisième Edition,* the undated Amsterdam reprint by Estienne Roger, from which the French quotation is taken.

particular key [*mode*]."[4] He added: "*Modular* est aussi sortir quelques fois hors du *Mode,* mais pour y rentrer à propos naturellement." Brossard's definition nicely points out the essential function of classical modulation — the deviation from a basic tonality, introduced for the sake of variety and expression, but necessarily followed presently by a return to what Tovey has referred to as the "home key."

While Mozart, the child prodigy, was taken on his North-European tour (1763-66), Jean-Jacques Rousseau finished his *Dictionnaire de Musique.*[5] The modern sense of modulation by now has won out. In the contemporary English translation of Rousseau's work[6] modulation is defined as "properly the method of establishing and treating the mode; but this word, at present, is more generally taken for the art of conducting the harmony, and the air successively in several modes, by a method agreeable to the ear and conformable to rules."

Although Rousseau somewhat naively acted as if he had just discovered the mysteries of modulation, the technique and artistic principle of modulation could then look back on a venerable history.

In the 15th and 16th centuries, modulations mostly meant changes of mode coupled with changes of key. A composer moving within the basic natural scale could form cadences on the tones of the tetrachord ascending from D to G; and, later, on the six tonics within the hexachord ascending from C to A. When the modes had converged towards the major and minor, and the Phrygian had become obsolete, only a pair of tonalities using the same basic scale (i.e., employing the same key signature) remained, forming the relation of a third between major and minor. This, as a matter of course, became a primary scheme of modulation. Not only does the sonata movement of the 18th century regularly move from an initial minor key to the relative major; but the movement in a major key shows a strong tendency to

[4] As translated by James Grassineau, *A Musical Dictionary,* London, 1740. A paragraph based on Brossard is followed here by a short discussion of modulation through the leading-tone. The book, "carefully abstracted from the best Authors in the *Greek, Latin, Italian, French,* and *English* Languages," is somewhat misleadingly classified in the Library of Congress as a translation of Brossard. A "new edition" appeared in Mozart's time (1769), with an "Appendix, selected from the Dictionnaire de Musique of M. Rousseau."

[5] Preface dated Dec. 20, 1764. Publ. Paris (and Geneva?), 1767, with date of 1768.

[6] *A Dictionary of Music, translated from the French of Mons. J. J. Rousseau,* by William Waring, London, n.d. A second ed. is dated 1779.

assign to the relative minor an important role in the development section. Mozart mostly obeyed fashion in both respects.

Occasionally the musician of the Renaissance ventured to introduce opposing modes on the same key. In the 17th century the use of opposing modes on the same key became quite popular, as Corelli's works show. It developed into a standard feature of the French suite, whence it moved into the minuet and trio. Haydn was particularly fond of its possibilities. Mozart used the contrast of major and minor on the same key less generously, but perhaps more profoundly. His attitude towards the device becomes evident in the opening of *Die Entführung aus dem Serail*. The Overture moves from the brilliant opening in C major to a rococo-oriental minor dominant. The *Andante* center-piece is in the tonic minor, but the material returns to form the opening aria in touchingly hopeful C major. Haydn's interchange of opposite modes on the same key frequently seems just playful; Mozart's rarely fails to suggest sweet melancholy or what Dowland might have called "cheerful tears." The opening movement of the Clarinet Quintet (K. 581; 1789) and the *Adagio ma non troppo* of the G-minor Quintet for strings (K. 516; 1787) contain unforgettable examples.

A third means of modulation was opened up in the late Renaissance by increasing use of *musica ficta,* in the sense of imaginary transpositions of the officially recognized hexachords of solmization. The addition of flats and sharps, before individual notes or as key signatures, introduced an increasing number of transposed modes, which meant changes of key without changes of mode. This led in due time to the exploration and description of the circle of fifths.

Lorenzo Penna included in a treatise on thorough-bass examples of a *Circolo, ò Ruota delle Cadenze,* a "circle or wheel of cadences" in continuous modulation, both ascending and descending by fifths.[7] The method was shown by Johann Kuhnau to Johann David Heinichen.[8] Heinichen designed the diagram of an improved *Musical Circle,*

---

[7] *Li primi albori musicali* (third book). The first publication, Bologna, 1672, was not available. In the "enlarged" ed. of 1679, the examples begin on p. 166. Cf. F. T. Arnold, *The Art of Accompaniment from a Thorough-Bass,* London, 1931, p. 147f.

[8] Heinichen, in his earlier treatise (see below, Note 9; p. 262) speaks of "Kircher's *Circulus per Quartas* or *per Quintas*" in a fashion that fits Penna's *circolo.* Athanasius Kircher had established a *Systema universale quo assumptum thema per XII. tonos mutatur essentialiter* (*Musurgia universalis,* Rome, 1650, II, 63f.), but

which contained all major and minor keys in alternation.[9] This was first published in 1711; and in 1728 Heinichen discussed the harmonic circle at great length, adding various samples of modulations — true or deceptive — through the entire circle of fifths.[10] From then on extensive modulation following the circle of fifths was a common tool of composition. Philipp Emanuel Bach, a generation later, referred to "the well-known musical circles," though adding a warning against the use of all twenty-four keys within the same piece.[11]

Modulations containing segments of the circle of fifths abound in Mozart's works. Descending modulations in fifths form the most frequent feature of his development sections. Obviously such modulations represented to him the easiest and most natural way of getting from one key to another. Ascending modulations in fifths are somewhat rarer and mostly less extended than the descending ones. A fascinating example, with which Mozart took particular pains, occurs in the last movement of the G-major Quartet, the first in the set dedicated to Haydn (K. 387; 1782).[12] Obviously Mozart never tired of modulations

---

the suggestion of continuous "mutation" in the circle of fifths does not seem to go back to him. Kuhnau, to whom Heinichen somewhat grudgingly gives credit in his later treatise (see below; p. 840f.), may well have shown Heinichen Kircher's tables and rounded out his explanation with the additional knowledge of the practical musician of the later 17th century.

[9] *Neu erfundene und gründliche Anweisung* etc., Hamburg, 1711, plate preceding p. 261; *Der General-Bass in der Composition, oder: Neue und gründliche Anweisung* etc., Dresden, 1728, plate preceding p. 837. The slightly more detailed later version is reproduced in Arnold (see Note 7), p. 268.

[10] Heinichen indicated that the omission of every other key turned his circle into a straight modulation ascending or descending by fifths, but he prided himself particularly on his ability to modulate through all the major and minor keys in succession. He also discussed modulation in continuous thirds, alternately major and minor, but disapprovingly pointed out the difficulty of modulation through a major third. For Mattheson's improvement of Heinichen's circle see Arnold, p. 277.

[11] *Versuch über die wahre Art das Clavier zu spielen,* Berlin, 1753 (2nd ed., 1759) and (second part) 1762. Reprint ed. W. Niemann, Leipzig, 1906, p. 124. Transl. by William J. Mitchell as *Essay on the True Art of Playing Keyboard Instruments,* New York, 1949, p. 435f.

[12] The modulation is accomplished by suspensions which resolve into the minor third of a tonic instead of the expected major third of a dominant. Thus Mozart moves from E minor to B-flat minor (actually A-sharp minor). The original form of the passage is given in Alfred Einstein's edition of Mozart's *The Ten Celebrated String Quartets,* London, n.d., pp. xviii and xxx-xxxi. Mozart canceled the original version and made two more sketches (one of these progressions only). All stages are reproduced in facsimile in Robert Haas, *Wolfgang Amadeus Mozart.* Potsdam, 1933, pp. 114-16.

following the circle of fifths, descending or ascending. But he invariably introduced several other principles of modulation in the course of a development section. However fond he was of the progression through fifths, he would not rely on this principle of procedure alone.

\*          \*

\*

Mozart's modulations are frequently carried by continuous bass-lines, ascending or descending diatonically, chromatically, or in mixed manner. The technique, intimately tied up with instrumental improvisation, considerably antedates the period under discussion. Heinichen referred to it,[13] and Philipp Emanuel Bach devoted the concluding chapter of his *Versuch* to it, under the heading *Von der freyen Fantasie*.[14] Philipp Emanuel indicated how a diatonic or chromatic bass-line might serve as the skeleton of an improvised fantasy, with the addition of pedalpoints and modulations, preferably suggested rather than carried out. The principles set forth in the *Versuch* can be traced in works by Philipp Emanuel Bach himself, his forerunners and followers. Mozart must have been familiar with Philipp Emanuel's book as well as his compositions, and his imagination was further stimulated by the treatment of bass-lines in certain works by Johann Sebastian Bach and Handel with which he became acquainted through Baron van Swieten.[15] At the prodding of Constanze, who took an unexpected delight in fugues, Mozart wrote his Fantasy and Fugue in C major (K. 394; 1782) as a deliberate re-creation of Baroque style. But he had outgrown the stage of direct imitation of models, and he abandoned his original plan to write half a dozen fantasies and fugues and to dedicate them to the baron.[16] Somewhat later, he explored the possibilities of continuous bass-lines in a monumental and daringly ingenious realization of his own, the Fantasy in C minor (K. 475; 1785), which was to

[13] *Der General-Bass* (see Note 9), pp. 901-16; specifically 903f.

[14] See Note 11. German reprint, *Zweyter Theil,* pp. 120-30, with example preceding p. 1; Mitchell's transl., "The Free Fantasia," pp. 430-45.

[15] See Alfred Einstein, *Mozart: His Character, His Work,* transl. by Arthur Mendel and Nathan Broder, New York, 1945, p. 150f.

[16] Mozart's letter to Nannerl, April 20, 1782, in *Briefe Wolfgang Amadeus Mozarts,* ed. Erich H. Müller von Asow, Berlin, 1942, II, 160f. Transl. by Emily Anderson in *The Letters of Mozart and His Family,* London, 1938, III, 1193-94. Mozart indicates that he wrote the fugue first and copied it while he was "thinking out" the *Praeludium.*

serve as an introduction to the Sonata in C minor (K. 457; 1784), written for his virtuoso pupil, Therese von Trattnern.[17]

The principle of continuous lines, particularly bass-lines, entered Mozart's regular composition as well. His extreme experiment in this field is the opening movement of the *Haffner Symphony* (K. 385; 1782). The main theme, which dominates the monothematic structure, begins with a diatonic measure-by-measure descent through a fourth. In the counter-exposition the line is extended through an octave. An ascending form, with a busy counterpoint underneath, figures prominently in the transition. Then the line descends through an eleventh, above a pedalpoint and below counterpoints that suggest the lyricism of a second subject. An ascending chromatic variation opens the closing group. The development begins in *piano* with an imitation between the ascending and descending forms; continues in *forte* with a similar imitation in contrary motion; and concludes, again in *piano,* with a sequential imitation in parallel motion.

Continuous lines occur conspicuously in introductory slow movements. The E-flat major Symphony (K. 543; 1788) starts, though this is rarely made clear in performance, with a slowly ascending bass-line which leads from the tonic with passing modulations to a pedalpoint on the dominant. More striking yet is the continuity of the bass in the fourth-movement *Adagio* of the G-minor Quintet. Aside from some initial imitations between first violin and 'cello, this is an arioso for solo violin with a throbbing accompaniment, suggesting a theatrical scene. After alternations of tonic and dominant the bass descends, first diatonically and then chromatically, through an octave (descending from D), with highly expressive modulatory feints. The broad final dominant opens into the concluding *Allegro.* The dramatic chiaroscuro of the *Adagio* makes the entry of the rondo finale in major particularly glowing.[18]

Ascending chromatic lines naturally carry modulations by ascending

[17] The Fantasy seems to have been written without key-signatures except for the sections in D major and B-flat major, but Mozart entered the beginning in his *Verzeichnüss aller meiner Werke* with the expected signature of three flats.

[18] G major is anticipated at the end of the *Adagio.* The turn is carried exclusively by the first violin. The major mode begins in most editions with E♮ at the end of the third measure before the double bar, which is probably the intended reading. The *Gesamtausgabe* of Mozart's works, however, replaces E♮ by an E♭. The newer of two Eulenburg miniature score editions, by Rudolf Gerber, neatly (and probably inadvertently) compromises between the two versions by starting the note in the measure mentioned as E♭ and changing to E♮ after the bar.

seconds, though of a particularly inconclusive, "passing" character. Such a chromatic ascent dominates the first part of the development in the *Andante* of the G-minor Symphony (K. 550; 1788). The section begins with a unison B♭, continuing the dominant sound from the end of the exposition. An unexpected C♭, heard first in unison (as E-flat minor VI), is harmonized as a subdominant of the tonic minor. B♭ and C♭ return; but C♭ is now followed, as if it had been a B♮, by C♮. Thus the ascent is set in motion. It leads through a fifth to F, suggesting deviations into D-flat major, E-flat major, and F minor. The expected continuation of the chromatic ascent through F♯ appears in a higher octave while the bass skips into A♭. Thus the continuity of the line is broken and an augmented-sixth formation results which points to the dominant of C minor, the relative of the home key. Considerable play, partly chromatic, establishes C minor as the outstanding key of the entire section, but the tonic never appears in a root position, and a measure-by-measure descent following the circle of fifths leads back, without retard, into E-flat major and to the recapitulation.

Philipp Emanuel suggested that in the modulations of the free fantasy "formal closing cadences are not always required; they are employed at the end and perhaps once in the middle. It suffices if the leading-tone of the key into which one moves is present in the bass or some other part, for this tone is the pivot and token of all natural modulations."[19] In the analysis of modulations it is of primary importance to recognize the degree of definiteness with which a given key is established. Mozart's, as well as Bach's, modulations cannot be understood if one refuses to acknowledge secondary dominants (dominants to chords other than the tonic), which add peculiar inflections to a scale without changing the basic tonality. But the essence of Mozart's, and Bach's, modulations is equally obscured if one tries to express all moves in terms of degrees of the original tonality. Mozart deliberately moves away from the basic key, establishing a conflict between the tonal area in which the music moves at a given point and the tonal area in which it might come to rest. The establishment and resolution of this conflict is a primary element of the musical action in sonata as well as in fugue.

Perhaps no work by Mozart displays as much gradation in the ren-

[19] Mitchell's translation (see Note 11), p. 434, with slight changes. See German ed., Part II, p. 123.

dition of key levels as the great C-minor Fantasy. The work is laid out in six large blocks. Freely modulating sections alternate with sections of stable tonality. The first and last sections (*Adagio* and *Tempo primo*) employ the same thematic materials, but changes in treatment and proportions make the opening section daringly modulatory while the concluding section is tonally static and strongly cadential. Against two closed-form sections with stable tonalities (D major and *Andantino* B-flat major) are set two more sections typical of the free fantasy. The first *Allegro* begins with phrases in A minor, G minor, and F major. While the bass descends steadily, successive keys are realized with increasing indefiniteness. At the end, tonality is dissolved to such an extent that the keys seem almost no more than colors added to the bass — a treatment that, while rare in Mozart, was to have a most significant future.

In the next modulatory section (marked *Più Allegro* following *Andantino*), tonalities are established with a different gradation of definiteness. The initial modulation establishes, clearly enough, G minor, F minor, E-flat minor, and D-flat major. Then the modulation descends in thirds: B-flat minor, G-flat major, E-flat minor. Each tonic is preceded by subdominant and dominant, but a broadly conceived cadence seems to accrue rather than a true modulation; and the continuation makes it clear that the formally, though quickly, established keys actually represent chords within D-flat major (I-VI-IV-II), which lead to a half-close in this key. Then the same principle is still more broadly applied. Emphatic modulation leads to F minor and then G minor. These represent the subdominant and dominant to C minor, and by turning the tonic of G minor into the dominant-seventh of C, the entire procedure becomes clearly the large-scale presentation of a cadence each chord-root of which is temporarily treated as a key level. This practice, too, occurred rarely in Mozart's works, but foreshadowed important later developments.

The opening section of the Fantasy touches upon D-flat major and reaches the expected dominant (G) only as a digression within B minor. The chromatic ascent C to D♭ is continued with the D major of the second section; and the chromatic descent C to B by the B-flat major of the fourth. Both patterns point towards E♭. In the course of the Fantasy, furthermore, all degrees of the scale are introduced at prominent points, with the exception of E♭ or E. The reason for this treatment is clear and yet extraordinarily subtle. The Fantasy was meant to precede the Sonata in C minor, which had been written previously. The Sonata, in regular fashion, concludes the opening exposition in E-flat major and includes a broad *Adagio* in the same key. Thus the order of the modulation in the Fantasy points beyond its boundaries to the composition that should follow it in performance.

\*      \*

\*

Sonata form was described by the contemporaries of Mozart, as Leonard Ratner has emphasized,[20] in terms of a differentiation of key relations. Theoretically speaking, sonata form provided two primary opportunities for modulation. The turn from the tonic to a closely related key within the exposition is generally carried out simply and directly. The initial abrogation of the tonic is frequently set forth with considerable display of activity, by Mozart as in the works of his forerunners. This impression of activity, however, is mostly accomplished by rhythmic means rather than modulatory thrusts. But Mozart, who was never satisfied with a well-established routine, occasionally offered a striking deviation, as in the sudden turns to the relative minor in the Piano Sonatas in F major (K. 332; 1778) and B-flat major (K. 570; 1789).

The recapitulation — to reverse the order of sections for the moment — could be presented without modulation at all, and was so presented by some of Mozart's predecessors. Mozart follows this method, for instance, in an earlier B-flat major Piano Sonata (K. 281; 1774). But such treatment meant that the recapitulation contained less action and therefore was less interesting than the exposition. Haydn solved the problem by an extraordinary play with false reprises (returns in wrong keys or at unexpected points) and by re-introducing the basic material of the exposition in different order and fashion. Mozart occasionally followed Haydn's example (as in the *Prague Symphony,* K. 504; 1786), but his recapitulations are mostly close replicas of the exposition. Yet he invariably managed to outdo the modulatory effect within the exposition by an elaborate counter-modulation in the recapitulation. A particularly charming example is the Overture to *Die Zauberflöte.* An interpolation of six measures carries out a conspicuous counter-modulation; where the regular run of the recapitulation is resumed, in the tonic instead of the previous dominant, the joint is made with a little run in the first violins which contains the only thirty-seconds and sixty-fourths of the entire

[20] *Harmonic Aspects of Classic Form,* in *Journal of the American Musicological Society,* II (1949), 158-68.

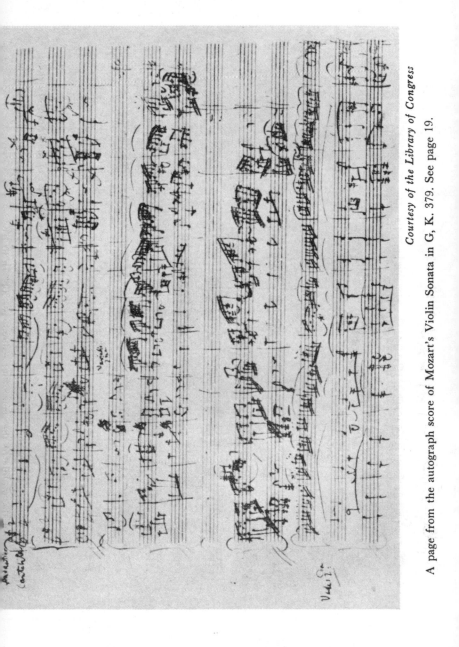

*Courtesy of the Library of Congress*

A page from the autograph score of Mozart's Violin Sonata in G, K. 379. See page 19.

*Courtesy of the British Museum*

Mozart's sketch for the finale of the Piano Quartet in E-flat, K. 493. See page 21. Beginning at measure 3 in the middle of the page: four canons. K. 508ᵃ (*e* to *h*).

*Mozart Museum, Salzburg*

Mozart's grand piano, made by Anton Walter of Vienna, *c.* 1780.
See page 80.

A page from Leopold Mozart's letter to his daughter, Vienna, Feb. 14, 1785. The three underscored lines near the bottom represent Haydn's famous remark about Wolfgang. See page 99.

*Allegro* — as elegant an emphasis on what Ralph Kirkpatrick has called "crux"[21] as can be found in musical literature.

The appointed field for the tournament of tonalities was, of course, the development section. The modulation back from the related key to the main key actually posed no problems. It could be accomplished quite simply, as it was in one of Mozart's early Piano Sonatas (G major, K. 283; presumably late in 1774), by a short play in the dominant key, which, over a pedalpoint, turns into the dominant chord. But the composers of the later 18th century increasingly seized upon the opportunity to contrast the second basic modulation in sonata form with the first. If the first modulation was made directly, the second was turned into a highly dramatic action of thrusts and feints. The composers who contributed most to the enlargement and intensification of the development section were, probably, Philipp Emanuel Bach and, unquestionably, Joseph Haydn.

Mozart's full maturity may be counted from approximately 1782, the time of *Die Entführung*, the *Haffner Symphony*, and the first of the quartets dedicated to Haydn. Haydn, though he developed more slowly than Mozart, had had a head-start of two dozen years, and had written by then some seventy-five symphonies and forty-odd quartets. Mozart did not merely inscribe his six quartets to Haydn, he devoted them to the older master and dear friend. Mozart showed that he had absorbed the technique of Haydn's latest quartets, the supremely original "Russian" Opus 33. But Mozart, at the same time, clearly meant to prove that he possessed a style and abilities of his own. Many details bear this out, from the chromaticism and the dynamic shadings of the opening *Allegro vivace assai* to the famous cross-relation at the beginning of the last quartet and beyond.

Mozart's development sections, as they crystallized in the "Haydn" Quartets, unfold as actions in several stages, each representing a different degree of key stability or a different principle of modulatory procedure. The tonalities most emphasized are, as a rule, closely related to the main key, no matter how far afield the transitory modulations seem to go.

The development of the first "Haydn" Quartet, in G major, is typical in plan. D major, E minor, and C major are established and abandoned in turn; the transition from the relative minor to the subdominant key is accomplished through a rapid descent in fifths. Then a slowly ascending chromatic bass-line supports modulation from F major

[21] *Domenico Scarlatti*, Princeton, 1953, p. 255f.

through D minor to E minor, where a full cadence is offered. A short ascent in fifths reaches the dominant key, which is likewise established with a complete cadence. The tonic of the dominant is turned into the dominant of the tonic, and the parts glide *calando* into the main tonic. The stages of modulation are clearly separated, elementary principles of transition are employed, and the keys emphasized (with symmetrical returns) are the closest relatives of the main key — the dominant, sub-dominant, and relative minor.

The extreme opposite to a regular organization of tonalities occurs in the Finale of the G-minor Symphony. It begins with an extraordinary modulatory thrust. An orchestral unison moves within eight measures, *Allegro assai,* from B-flat through F minor, C minor, G minor, D minor, into A minor. Each of these keys is established only by a leading-tone and the third of the tonic. The keys follow each other so precipitously and they are established so precariously that the modulation remains utterly unconvincing. Such arbitrary and sudden changes of key occa-sionally occur in Mozart's development sections, particularly at the start. They invariably produce strong modulatory tension, for a key so boldly and unsatisfactorily gained cannot be maintained.

Mozart proceeds to allay the uncertainty just aroused. The modula-tion in ascending fifths is promptly rescinded by a somewhat broader descent in fifths. But while the ascent took in five fifths, the descent covers only four; and thus the entire procedure has netted the ascent of a fifth, from B♭ to F.

Now a different principle of modulation enters. A harmonic sequence leads from F minor to E-flat major; and through a typical third-relation C minor is gained. The modulation so far has led from B♭ through F to C — to reach the tonic, only a third ascent of a fifth is needed.

But Mozart once more goes out of his way. Fast modulations begin another ascent through the circle of fifths. Now seven fifths are covered. The ascent ends in C-sharp minor, and this key is most generously em-phasized. Yet, the increasingly definite cadences fail to reach a tonic: the last of three deceptive endings produces a dominant to F-sharp minor, and once more an inordinately fast ascent in the circle of fifths is counteracted by a corresponding descent. But this time Mozart has ascended through seven fifths and descended through six. He has gained his third ascending fifth and may, after a brief halt on the dominant, embark on the recapitulation.

The ingenuity of this plan has remained unequaled. The development unfolds in three stages, each of which carries the modulation a fifth upward: and yet the final dominant is reached from above. The first and third stages are accomplished in the same manner while the second one introduces a contrasting principle. The last stage brings into play the largest range of keys; and the key most emphatically presented, C-sharp minor, is, within the circle of fifths, the true antipode to the tonic, G minor.

Each of the mature Mozart's development sections presents an individual organization of tonalities, and their variety is stunning. Abundant proof of this is offered by the two other symphonic finales Mozart wrote in the summer of 1788.[22]

The development of the E-flat major Finale flashes by with continuous deceit. Five times within its short course is a major chord or key replaced by the tonic minor. Three times in succession is a modulation to the major third below carried out. After the B-flat major close of the exposition, the modulation begins with an unexpected G-major run, which is clarified as a dominant to C minor. The descent by thirds leads through A♭ to E (which is really F♭) and hence to C (which is really D♭♭). C minor is treated to a tonal cycle and half-close. Then the G-major run of the beginning is heard again, now introduced as a dominant, but continued as a tonic. A common-tone modulation turns the last tonic of the section, D minor, into the proper dominant to E-flat major.

The development of the *Jupiter* Finale, to the contrary, faithfully follows regular procedure almost to the end. The initial dominant leads, through a touch of C, to the relative minor. Then a broad modulation in the circle of fifths descends as far as the subdominant,

[22] The frequently made statement that Mozart composed his last three symphonies "in six consecutive weeks" (so in Donald Francis Tovey's *Essays in Musical Analysis,* Vol. I, London, since 1935, frequently reprinted, p. 186) should be modified. Mozart seems to have added date and name to his scores and entered the works in his *Verzeichnüss* when the composition was completed. When he started work on the E-flat Symphony cannot be ascertained. The fact that Mozart entered three additional compositions under the same date as the symphony (June 26) may suggest that he imagined these while he wrote out the symphony (see Note 16). It can be assumed rather safely, on the other hand, that the G-minor Symphony was written between June 26 and July 25, the date of entry; and the *Jupiter* between July 25 and August 10. The composition time for the G minor is further narrowed down by the fact that Mozart could enter in his musical diary three more works between July 10 and 16.

F major. A counter-move ascends through the circle of fifths as far as E minor, which is pointed up by a half-close. A modulation over a descending chromatic bass leads back to the tonic with such unseemly speed that considerable tension remains. The recapitulation shortly begins to modulate again: from C through D minor to E minor and back through D minor to C major. The composition student of the 18th century was unquestionably warned not to return in such fashion to a key that he had just managed to quit; and Mozart did not fail to demonstrate this gawky method in his parody on bad composing and playing, *Ein musikalischer Spass* (K. 522; 1787).[23] But in the *Jupiter* Finale the modulation bridges the gap between C and E that the development had left open, and thus the circular tour becomes eminently meaningful — particularly since the same esthetic principle was prominently displayed in the development of the first movement.

\*   \*

\*

Key relationships, however fascinating in themselves, cannot be separated from the thematic material which supports, and is supported by, the modulations. In Haydn's earlier quartets the thematic material is increasingly subject to the most entertaining elaboration. The process was completed with the "Russian" Quartets. Haydn generously worked out thematic bits in his expositions and recapitulations; and he matched the intensity of continuous key-changes in the development section by equally continuous and intense thematic elaboration. Mozart was more inclined to display in the outer sections of sonata form a variety of themes and styles, but for the inner section he wholeheartedly adopted the principle established by Haydn. Thus his development sections are somewhat more definitely differentiated from exposition and recapitulation than Haydn's.

The development section may open, like the second part of a true binary form, with a reference to the initial theme. In comparatively few instances only does this theme begin in the key in which the exposition ended (Piano Sonata in A minor, K. 310; 1778), and it is apt

[23] Here the development of the opening *Allegro* begins in the dominant, C major, with an alternation of V 6 and I in *forte*. Then follows, in *piano* and entirely disconnected, a full cadence in B-flat major, beginning with the subdominant chord. B-flat major is confirmed, in *forte*, by another alternation of V 6 and I. This is followed, again in sudden *piano*, by a full cadence in A minor, beginning with the subdominant chord. The next measure presents B-flat major once more, in *forte*. This is treated as a subdominant to the home key, but the memory of a "modulation" through B-flat major — A minor — B-flat major remains.

to be subject to modulatory variation before long. More frequently Mozart simply re-introduces his subject abruptly in a new, wrong-sounding key, a method of which Haydn, too, was fond. The more unexpected the key, the stronger seems to be the urge to return to the proper key and thus the need of further modulation. In the unique E-flat major Divertimento for three strings (K. 563; 1788), the B-flat major ending of the exposition is followed, without apology, by a thematic G-major triad, heard as the dominant to the relative minor. This modulatory impetus leads within six measures to F-sharp minor (the relative minor to the antipode of the home key) and within eight more to B-flat major, the dominant from which the development should have started — at which point a fresh modulatory impulse is gained by an interchange of modes.

Mozart clearly was not motivated by the concept that a development section should elaborate all of the material presented in the exposition, although his piano concertos establish such precedents. As a rule the initial theme is generously worked out. When it appears at the beginning of the development section, it is not likely to be discarded soon. When it fails to appear at this point, it is usually brought into play in the further course of the section. A second principal subject, on the other hand, suggests lyrical treatment in a stable tonality and is therefore not suitable for a basically modulatory section. The second subject accordingly is mostly avoided in Mozart's sonata developments. But occasionally a lyrical segment of the second-theme group is quoted within the development section, as in the first movement of the last E-flat major Symphony.

Intermediary thematic material from the exposition recurs in the development with considerable variance of extent and great diversity of treatment. Particularly generous in the elaboration of diverse motifs from the exposition is the development of the *Allegro* of the *Prague Symphony*. A unique solution is offered in the B-flat major Sonata, K. 570, in which the modulation to the dominant is largely carried by a subsidiary theme while the first subject, with a new counterpoint, serves in lieu of a second principal subject. Here the entire transition returns as the opening half of the development, beginning with the last measure of the exposition as a metrical start and carrying out a different modulation with identical material. The second half of the section elaborates the principal subject, with its counterpoint.

Quite frequent, finally, is the elaboration of material from the very end of the exposition, again in accordance with Haydnesque models.

In the first movement of the *Jupiter* the returning material is a complete closing theme, but Mozart is more partial to terse motifs. In the first *Allegro* of the E-flat major Symphony an ornamental pattern is used both before the entry of the second subject and with the final dominant chord of the exposition; the same pattern raises the curtain for the development and later is subject to considerable imitative play. Outdoing Haydn, Mozart in certain cases uses the closing motif as a foil for violent changes of key, after which the motif is discarded in favor of more prominent thematic material. As a result, the measures built of the closing motifs sound like an extension of the exposition, and the development seems to begin in a remote key. Thus the E-flat major development follows the dominant with the relative minor and then turns to the subdominant; the entry of the second subject in A-flat major is actually heard as if it were the true opening of the section. The last Piano Sonata (D major, K. 576; 1789) similarly takes up the closing motif with which the A-major dominant was presented at the end of the exposition. Two varied repetitions lead through common-tone modulations of Schubertian flavor to B-flat major. In this key, then, the first subject returns and the true development begins.

Mozart's mature development sections primarily work out material from the exposition, but with complementary additions. The new material is mostly of modest thematic scope, representing motifs rather than broad subjects, or extensions and standard figures rather than clear-cut motifs. In rare instances, however, an entirely new theme enters in the development section. The exceptionally busy exposition of the "Hunt" Quartet (B-flat major, K. 458; 1784) is contrasted at the beginning of the development with a quiet pastoral melody of utter metrical regularity and harmonic simplicity, effecting a prolonged stay in the dominant key. The homogeneity of the nearly monothematic and highly chromatic *Allegro non troppo* with which Mozart concluded his next Quartet (A major, K. 464; 1785)[24] is similarly counterbalanced by the introduction of a new subject in the development section, a hymn-like theme that unfolds shortly before the conclusion of the

[24] The E-flat major Quartet, K. 428, was composed in June or July 1783 as the third of the "Haydn" Quartets, but entitled *Quartetto IV* in Mozart's holograph and published as Op. 10, No. 4. The "Hunt" Quartet, though composed later, was identified as *Quartetto III* and accordingly appeared as Op. 10, No. 3. The *Gesamtausgabe* and other modern editions present the quartets in strictly chronological order, but the arrangement envisaged by Mozart himself displays a subtler sequence of moods and a more logical succession of tonalities (G major — D minor; B-flat major — E-flat major). Einstein, in his edition of Mozart's later quartets (see Note 12), restores Mozart's own "well-considered" order.

modulatory action and carries out a modicum of modulation. The *dolce* F-major theme in the D-major Divertimento for strings and horns (K. 334; 1779) reflects the looser texture of the genre.

Materials without thematic stature function in a few, particularly effective instances as modulatory props at the onset of the development, in a fashion similar to the closing motifs just described. The exposition of the G-minor Symphony, first movement, returns from the relative B-flat major to the tonic by a single chord, a dominant-seventh with F♯ on top. In the repeat of the exposition this leading-tone is not resolved in the same octave. At the beginning of the development, it is; and a sequential G♯ points towards A minor. The expected tonic is contained in a chain of slowly descending thirds in the woodwinds, reminiscent of the descent above which the counter-exposition of the opening theme had entered. The descent replaces the expected C by C♯ and lands in F-sharp minor, in which key the theme re-enters and the thematic elaboration begins. The same chain of descending thirds in the woodwinds appears in the Finale, where it is entirely unrelated to the thematic material of the movement, but serves as a tenuous bridge between the largely athematic opening ascent and the thematic first descent in the circle of fifths. The most pointedly bare non-thematic modulation, finally, appears in the development of the first movement of the *Jupiter*. Open woodwind octaves lead from the dominant G through F and B♭ to E♭, where harmony re-enters and thematic work-out begins. Modulatory tension could not be established with greater effect or economy.

\* \*
\*

When Mozart began to write the "Haydn" Quartets, he was just passing through a phase of intense preoccupation with counterpoint. While he soon abandoned his exercises in Baroque style, the renewed contact with Baroque models proved immensely fruitful. Henceforth Mozart profusely introduced contrapuntal designs into his instrumental compositions. But contrapuntal treatment is frankly subordinate to thematic play and harmonic progression, and thus even the most striking contrapuntal features avoid the stigma of seeming "learned." Haydn, whose interest in counterpoint was reflected in the Quartets Op. 20, concluded three of these quartets with fugues. Mozart's answer was the fusion of fugue and sonata in the last movement of the first "Haydn" Quartet. The synthesis succeeded so well that Mozart could rely on it for the vastly expanded *Jupiter* Finale.

The range of thematic material that Mozart is willing to introduce in a development section is limited, but the material is subject to an unlimited diversity of treatment. The wonderful richness of this variety is achieved by thematic variation, sequential or free extension, and the minute gradation of contrapuntal density. Mozart thus could realize a modulatory scheme in innumerable ways. Which, then, did he choose?

Mozart's modulations, it has been suggested, are carried out in several succeeding stages. These stages are generally accomplished with basically different material. The descent in fifths in the *Jupiter* Finale is wrought from interlocking appearances of a closing motif. Where the direction of the modulation reverts, the main theme re-enters to remain predominant until the final key is reached. The three stages of the first "Haydn" Quartet movement are almost as clearly carried by different materials — an extended variant of the main theme, a motif introduced as an extension to the main theme, and free material that does not crystallize into definite motifs. In addition, the two complete cadences within the section quote the thematically independent cadence formula with which the exposition so strikingly concluded.

Together with the thematic material, the treatment changes. The pivot in the *Jupiter* Finale sets *piano* against *forte;* non-imitative counterpoint against lively imitations; and woodwinds alone against other sonorities. Thus the change in modulatory treatment coincides with changes in at least three different aspects of music. In the "Haydn" Quartet, the stages of modulation are similarly realized in clearly differentiated styles: almost rhapsodic solos for single instruments; strict imitations over steady accompaniment rhythms; and sequential or freely melodic soprano lines.

Even where the thematic material is maintained, any change in the modulatory procedure is paralleled by changes in the thematic treatment. Once more the C-minor Fantasy may serve as a prime example. The opening movement is founded on a continuous bass-line, but it moves in strangely irregular fashion. The line descends chromatically from C to A♭, rests on A♭, then ascends to B (or rather C♭), and descends, again chromatically, to G♭, which is enharmonically changed into F♯. Here new material enters, and the rest of the section is given over to an oscillation between F♯ and G. Each change in the direction of the line occurs simultaneously with other changes. To describe only one of these, the turn of direction on B sees the main motif inverted and moved from the soprano to the bass, omits an expected *forte* at the beginning of the measure, and replaces an Alberti-bass figure with a repeated-sixteenth-note pattern. The movement displays an extraordinary irregularity of bass-line progression as well as chord progression, but each deflection is so fully supported by corresponding changes in other elements that the result is an impression not of wilfulness but of mysterious profundity.

The musical composition is built up of many elements, forming groups such as melody, harmony, rhythm, counterpoint, sonority, texture, and structure. These elements behave according to their own laws, and they are, in principle, independent of each other. But elements can be coordinated through synchronous changes in treatment. This principle is beautifully illuminated at the beginning of the first *Jupiter* development. The section begins, as was indicated before, with an abrupt turn from G to E♭, not supported by thematic material. Thus a modulatory gap is formed. E-flat major is broadly presented, with a return of the closing theme. A sudden *forte* introduces nearly canonic imitation of the concluding measure of the theme, at a measure's distance, between upper and lower strings. Modulation leads from E-flat major through F minor to G minor. Here the direction of the modulation turns: G minor is followed by F minor and then, again, E-flat major. The composer has returned to his point of departure, but he has bridged the original gap between G minor and E-flat major, and he has convincingly modulated into E-flat major, making two irregularities justify each other. Now, where the direction of the modulation changes, the imitation between upper and lower strings changes from a measure's distance to one of half a measure. Certainly no direct relation can be established between a reversion of modulatory direction and a shortening of imitatory distance. But since the changes of the elements coincide, an illusion of inner sympathy between the elements is created which is profoundly satisfying.

Synchronism of changes reaches its acme in the thoroughly monothematic Finale of the G-minor Symphony. The initial upward thrust is mainly athematic. It is carried by all strings and woodwinds in unison, *forte*. The alternating thirds and leading-tones are unevenly spaced; thus for once a sequential modulation is contradicted by its supporting rhythm. The arbitrariness of the rhythmic organization emphasizes the modulatory "unformality" — to use a word from Thomas Morley's vocabulary. The result is an impression of utter wilfulness and truly dramatic tension. But from this point on the elements are perfectly integrated. The first descent in fifths is carred out in *piano*, with imitations of the principal head-motif between the violins and woodwinds. The turn from F minor to C minor reintroduces *forte* and the horns, while temporarily eliminating the woodwinds. The theme, extended, serves as material for a fugato with two paired imitations. The second, broader ascent in fifths employs the four string parts in continuous imitation, with reinforcement of each successive tonic and leading-tone in the woodwinds. The passage in C-sharp minor opposes woodwind choir and string choir in antiphonal imitations. The last attempt at a cadence in C-sharp minor blooms out of a sudden *piano*. The final descent in fifths, beginning with the deceptive close, once more presents continuous imitations in two parts, but now the high strings are coupled with the bassoons, and the low strings with the high woodwinds, in unusually forceful octave-writing. Thus each phase of the modulation appears in an entirely different texture. Although the main motif is continuously present, an extraordinary diversity is accomplished, and complete coordination of the changes in modulatory procedures and the changes in thematic treatment is achieved.

The coordination of changes deserves to be recognized as a primary principle of musical esthetics. Its effects can be traced in the relations between rhythm and melodic shape in the classical counterpoint of the 16th century. But no period has carried out the principle as faithfully as the late 18th century, and no composer has done so as ingeniously as Mozart.

Where several musical elements are subject to change of treatment at the same moment, an inner relation between the elements is established that is not inherent in their essential qualities. A modulatory plan can be easily imagined as thought up by a human intellect, but a multiple sympathy between various aspects of music seems to suggest that a deeper force is at work.

A simile might help to clarify this statement. Out of a tulip bulb will grow a flower all parts of which come in groups of three or, seemingly, six. The seeds of a plant of the Crucifer family are likely to develop flowers in which all elements are represented in pairs or double pairs. There is no need for any plant to produce the same number of sepals, petals, stamens, and parts of pistil and ovary, but that is how Nature works in her regular manifestations; and it seems cosmically logical that parts dominated by the same set of numbers should have grown out of the same germinating cell.

Musical elements, when subject to a common law, similarly seem to transcend the human mind. A fully integrated piece of music ceases to appear as *composed*, "put together" out of its constitutive elements — it seems to have grown like a product of nature. "Imitation of nature" was still one of the avowed aims of the composer in Mozart's time. In his coordination of disparate musical elements Mozart certainly did not consciously imitate nature — he paralleled nature's actions. This marks the peculiar character and outstanding accomplishment of Mozart's genius. Its transcendent significance shines forth from many of his mature works and with particularly exciting brilliance from Mozartean modulations.

# MOZART AND THE "CLAVIER"*

## By NATHAN BRODER

"V ERY GREAT CONFUSION exists on the subject of the harpsichord, the clavichord, the spinet, and the pianoforte," wrote Mme. Wanda Landowska more than thirty years ago.[1] Much of the confusion remains, and its clouds seem especially dense about the clavier music of Mozart. During his brief lifetime the brilliant career of the harpsichord faded swiftly, while the piano sprang from obscurity to dominance. During that same short period the clavichord achieved its greatest popularity — a popularity confined, to be sure, to Central Europe. Which of these instruments did Mozart have in mind when he wrote a particular concerto, or sonata, or trio, or song? One looks in vain in Abert or Wyzewa and Saint-Foix for any definite information on this point.

It is, in fact, impossible to say with certainty for which of the stringed keyboard instruments some of the clavier works were intended; but as regards most of them — including many of the most important —, the answer seems clear. And perhaps some light can be thrown on the former group by consideration of a few facts that have hitherto been given insufficient attention.     *     *

*

Let us see what is known about Mozart's relationships with the three main types of instruments — the harpsichord, the clavichord, and the piano. The first (named also, according to the language employed, *clavecin, Flügel, cembalo* or *clavicembalo,*[2] and *clavecimbael*) was, of course, during most of Mozart's life, the predominant keyboard instru-

---

*Although this essay was written in 1941, its main points are still valid, and it is reprinted unchanged.—*Editor.*

[1] Wanda Landowska, *La Musique ancienne,* 2nd ed., 1909, p. 194.

[2] The second number on the program for the concert Mozart gave in Mantua on January 16, 1770, is a *"Concerto di Gravecembalo"* and the fourth a *"Sonata di Cembalo".* (Otto Jahn, *W. A. Mozart,* Vol. I [1856], p. 187.) This would seem to support the claim of some writers that *"gravecembalo"* referred to an instrument with a larger compass than that of the *clavicembalo* or *cembalo,* and was not merely another name for the same thing.

ment, in the opera house,[3] in the concert hall, and — especially in its smaller form, the spinet — in the home. The Mozart family owned a large instrument, with two manuals, made by Christian Ernst Friederici of Gera.[4] Possibly they had a spinet also.[5]

The clavichord is seldom mentioned in any discussion of the influences that affected Mozart's style of writing for the keyboard. But it is not unlikely that this instrument had a large share in determining that style. Leopold Mozart must have been aware of the great importance attached to the clavichord by C. P. E. Bach and other eminent musicians of the time, especially for teaching correct performance to the young. Bach wrote:

> Whoever can play the clavichord well will be able to do the same on the harpsichord also, but not *vice versa*. One must therefore employ the clavichord for learning good performance, and the harpsichord for acquiring the requisite strength in the fingers.[6]

The popularity of the clavichord was greatest in North and Central Germany,[7] but the instrument seems to have found a place in many households in South Germany and Austria also. We know that there was one in the Mozart home at least as early as 1769, when Wolfgang was thirteen,[8] and that he played on clavichords in Augsburg and Mannheim in 1777, and in Linz in 1783;[9] and a report from Dresden in 1789 mentions that "his skill on the clavichord and the fortepiano is indescribable".[10] A clear indication of his attitude towards the instrument is given in a letter from his father, April 13-20, 1778:

[3] The piano may have entered the opera house while Mozart was still alive. A piano with a built-in conductor's stand has survived from "the end of the 18th century". "Such instruments were used by opera conductors to accompany secco-recitative." (Georg Kinsky, *Musikhistorisches Museum von Wilhelm Heyer in Cöln. Katalog*, Vol. I [1910], p. 137.)

[4] See Leopold Mozart's letters of Dec. 8, 1763, and Nov. 13, 1777, in Emily Anderson, "The Letters of Mozart and his Family", 1938, Vol. I, p. 45; Vol. II, p. 537.

[5] They definitely had one if the Stein *"clavierl"* mentioned in Leopold's letter of Aug. 20, 1763, and in Wolfgang's letter of Oct. 3, 1778, is the same as the *"Spinettel"* mentioned by Constanze in a letter of June 13, 1810.

[6] *Versuch über die wahre Art das Clavier zu spielen*, Part I, 1753, p. 11. See also the citations from Virdung, Praetorius, Mattheson, Walther, Marpurg, and others in Cornelia Auerbach, *Die deutsche Clavichordkunst des 18. Jahrhunderts*, 1930, pp. 9f., 46 ff.

[7] Auerbach, p. 61.

[8] "In a fit of absentmindedness I took away with me on my watch the key of our clavichord." Leopold Mozart to his wife, in Anderson, Vol. I, p. 148.

[9] Anderson, Vol. II, pp. 460, 495, 540; Vol. III, p. 1281.

[10] *Musikalische Real-Zeitung*, 1789, p. 191.

If you could find in Paris a good clavichord, such as we have, you would no doubt prefer it and it would suit you better than a harpsichord.[11]

After he was married Mozart had a clavichord of his own, on which, according to Constanze, he played and composed a great deal.[12]

Since the fingers have almost direct control of the metal tangents that strike the strings, a good clavichord in the hands of an expert player is capable of a sustained singing tone,[13] it allows innumerable gradations of tone within a limited range of dynamics (*ppp* to *mf* according to modern standards),[14] and it permits the nicest of phrasing. It seems reasonable to suppose that it was familiarity with such an instrument from infancy on that predisposed Mozart towards the piano — in many ways and except for its lack of the *Bebung* a clavichord of greater dynamic range and power —, and that accounts partly for his expressive playing of both the harpsichord and the piano.

It is commonly thought that Mozart had little to do with the piano until he visited Johann Andreas Stein in Augsburg in 1777. But there is reason to believe that, though pianos were by no means plentiful before the last quarter of the century, he had heard about them, seen them, and even occasionally played upon them since his early childhood. Stein made a piano for the Archbishop of Salzburg probably before Mozart was born.[15] Leopold Mozart, the author of the *Violinschule,* undoubtedly

[11] Anderson, Vol. II, p. 781.

[12] Arthur Schurig, *Konstanze Mozart. Briefe, Aufzeichnungen, Dokumente,* 1922, p. 96. Constanze bequeathed it to her sons, one of whom, Karl, eventually presented it to the Mozarteum in Salzburg. This instrument has started a little game of errors of its own. Where Constanze writes *"Clavier"*, Schurig, in his explanatory footnotes, calls the instrument once a *"Spinett"* and another time a *"Klavichord (Spinett)"*. This latter mistake appeared also in an early catalogue of the Mozarteum, and led Mme. Landowska to write: "Mozart never availed himself of either the clavichord or the spinet. I have not yet had the pleasure of visiting the Mozarteum, but I can assert that this instrument must be a square piano." (*La Musique ancienne,* p. 195.) In the 1931 edition of the Mozarteum catalogue the instrument is called simply a *"Clavichord"*, which is what Constanze called it in her will. (Schurig, *op. cit.,* p. 127.) For a picture of Mozart's piano, see illustrations between pages 64-5.

[13] *Cf.* Leopold Mozart's letter to Wolfgang, Nov. 13, 1777: "[Herr Pfeil] has a clavichord also in mahogany, which he would not sell for 200 gulden, as he says that this instrument simply has not got its equal; that the descant sounds like a violin being played softly, and the bass notes like trombones." (Anderson, Vol. II, p. 537. We have substituted "trombones" for Miss Anderson's "trumpets"; the German version has *"Posaunen"*.)

[14] Erwin Bodky, *Der Vortrag alter Klaviermusik,* 1932, p. 21.

[15] In Stein's list of instruments he finished after coming to Augsburg in 1750, there is an entry reading:

Forte P. Erzbischof Salzb. 200.-

Eva Hertz, *Johann Andreas Stein,* 1937, p. 93.

knew Quantz's *Versuch einer Anweisung die Flöte traversiere zu spielen*. Quantz was one of the earliest champions of the piano, and the elder Mozart could hardly have ignored a passage like the following, which, in 1752, probably startled musicians and perhaps even seemed exaggerated:

> Everything required [for accompaniment] can be executed most conveniently on a pianoforte, for this instrument, more than any others that are called "clavier", has in itself most of the attributes that are necessary for proper accompaniment; and this depends exclusively upon the player and his judgment. The same is true, indeed, of a good clavichord, as regards playing, but not as regards effect, for the *fortissimo* is lacking.[16]

Only ten years later C. P. E. Bach wrote concerning the clavier as an accompanying instrument:

> The fortepiano and the clavichord support best a performance in which the finest nuances of taste appear.[17]

The piano was not unknown in London when the Mozart family lived there in 1764 and 1765 and the nine-year-old Wolfgang fraternized with Johann Christian Bach, who is said to have preferred that instrument to the harpsichord.[18] The first actual evidence we have of Mozart playing on a piano is a report in Schubart's *Deutsche Chronik* for 1775, in which a correspondent from Munich writes:

> Last winter in Munich I heard two of the greatest clavier players, Herr Mozart and Herr Captain von Beecke. My host, Herr Albert, who is an enthusiast for the great and the beautiful, has an excellent fortepiano at home. There I heard these two giants compete on the clavier.[19]

In 1777 Mozart called upon Stein in Augsburg, played on his pianos, and wrote a famous and oft-quoted letter, part of which we may perhaps be forgiven for printing once more:

> This time I shall begin at once with Stein's pianofortes. Before I had seen any of his make, Späth's claviers had always been my favourites. But now I much prefer Stein's, for they damp ever so much better than the Regensburg instruments. ... In whatever way I touch the keys, the tone is always even. It never jars, it is never stronger or weaker or entirely absent; in a word, it is always even. It is true that he does not sell a pianoforte of this kind for less than three hundred gulden, but the trouble and the labour which Stein puts into the making of it cannot be paid for. His instruments have this special advantage over others that they are made with escape action. Only one maker in a hundred bothers about this. But

---

[16] *Versuch...*, 1752, new ed. 1906, p. 175.

[17] *Versuch...*, Part II, 1762, p. 2.

[18] "Grove's Dictionary of Music and Musicians", 4th ed., Vol. IV, p. 154.

[19] *Deutsche Chronik, Jahrg. 2* (1775), p. 267. This report is wrongly attributed to Schubart himself, writing in the *Chronik* for 1776, in Abert (*W. A. Mozart*, Vol. I, 1923, p. 369).

without an escapement it is impossible to avoid jangling and vibration after the note is struck. When you touch the keys, the hammers fall back again the moment after they have struck the strings, whether you hold down the keys or release them. ... He guarantees that the sounding-board will neither break nor split. When he has finished making one for a clavier, he places it in the open air, exposing it to rain, snow, the heat of the sun and all the devils in order that it may crack. Then he inserts wedges and glues them in to make the instrument very strong and firm. He is delighted when it cracks, for he can then be sure that nothing more can happen to it. Indeed he often cuts into it himself and then glues it together again and strengthens it in this way.... The device too which you work with your knee is better on his than on other instruments. I have only to touch it and it works; and when you shift your knee the slightest bit, you do not hear the least reverberation.[20]

Little is known about Franz Jacob Späth's pianos except that they were highly praised by such contemporary writers as Schubart and Forkel.[21] There is nothing to indicate that Mozart actually owned a Späth instrument, as has been claimed; but the whole passage points to a previous knowledge of the piano, a knowledge that was far from superficial.

Pianos must have been comparatively rare in Salzburg, but Mozart found them "everywhere"[22] in Mannheim in 1777 as well as in Paris the next year. And from the first days of his permanent settling-down in Vienna to the end of his life the piano was plainly the stringed keyboard instrument he played on by choice. We know that he used a piano at his first public concert as a mature artist in Vienna, on April 3, 1781[23] — probably a Stein borrowed from Countess Thun. Sometime between the beginning of 1782 and 1785 Mozart acquired a piano of his own, an instrument made by Anton Walter of Vienna about 1780 and now in the Mozart Museum in Salzburg. In a letter of March 12, 1785, Leopold Mozart writes to his daughter from Vienna:

Since my arrival your brother's fortepiano has been taken at least a dozen times to the theatre or to some other house. He has had a large fortepiano pedal made, which is under the instrument and is about two feet longer and extremely heavy. It is taken to the Mehlgrube every Friday and has also been taken to Count Zichy's and to Prince Kaunitz's.[24]

[20] Anderson, Vol. II, p. 478 ff.

[21] Heinrich Herrmann, *Die Regensburger Klavierbauer Späth und Schmahl und ihr Tangentenflügel,* 1928, p. 21.

[22] "Everyone thinks the world of Wolfgang, but indeed he plays quite differently from what he used to in Salzburg—for there are pianofortes everywhere here, on which he plays so extraordinarily well that people say they have never heard the like." Mozart's mother to his father, in Anderson, Vol. II, p. 644. (We have added the word "everywhere" ["*überall*" appears in the German version]. )

[23] See the facsimile of the announcement in Robert Haas, *Wolfgang Amadeus Mozart,* 1933, p. 26.

[24] Anderson, Vol. III, p. 1325.

The titles of Mozart's clavier works are not very helpful towards the solution of our problem. Almost all the individual works of this sort specifically mentioned in the family correspondence are referred to as for *"Clavier"*. It is obvious that the Mozarts invariably employ this term in its generic sense, though it was otherwise often used in the second half of the 18th century to mean only "clavichord".[25] In the thematic catalogue of his own works that he kept from 1784 on, Wolfgang uses only *"Klavier"*.[26] The evidence of the musical MSS would seem to indicate that it was Mozart's lifelong habit usually to write *"Cembalo"* (sometimes *"Clavicembalo"*), if he named the keyboard instrument at all. *"Pianoforte"* occasionally appears from about 1782 on, but he continues to use *"Cembalo"* during the last decade, when, as we shall see, he can mean by it only the piano.

The first editions of those of Mozart's works that were published during his lifetime also throw little light on our problem. As early as 1763, Johann Gottfried Eckard wrote in the preface to his own Op. 1, *6 Sonates pour le Clavecin:*

> I have endeavored to render this work equally useful for the harpsichord, the clavichord, and the pianoforte [*forté et piano*]. It is for this reason that I have felt obliged to indicate so often the soft and loud passages, which would have been useless if I had had only the harpsichord in view.[27]

With the growing popularity of the piano, publishers took no chances of losing the business of owners of either the new instrument or the old. Of 109 items for or with clavier reviewed or announced in the first volume of Cramer's *Magazin der Musik* (published in 1783 and covering publications from 1779-83), 60 are for *"Clavecin ou Pianoforte"*, 27 for *"Clavecin"*, 12 for *"Clavier"* (clavichord), 5 for *"Pianoforte"*, 2 for *"Clavier oder Fortepiano"*, 1 for *"Clavichord"*, 1 for *"Clavier, Clavecin oder Pianoforte"*, and 1 is a concerto for harpsichord *and* pianoforte.[28] From about 1778 most of Mozart's publications for or with clavier issued during his lifetime are *"pour le Clavecin ou le Pianoforte"*.

The compass of a particular work does not necessarily indicate a particular instrument. The standard range of all the instruments we are

[25] Auerbach, p. 44 f.

[26] *Wolfgang Amadé Mozart, Verzeichnis aller meiner Werke.* Facsimile edition by O. E. Deutsch, 1938.

[27] Hertz, p. 28 f.

[28] "Herr J. C. Kellner announces a quite new double concerto for a harpsichord and piano forte or 2 harpsichords with the accompaniment of 2 violins, 2 flutes, 2 horns, viola, and bass, in F major . . ." Cramer, Vol. I, p. 520.

concerned with was, during the greater part of Mozart's lifetime, five octaves, from FF to f''''.[29] And Mozart never exceeds these limits.[30]

Eckard's preface, however, yields a clue that proves useful when applied to the works of Mozart: Where the original MS, or a first edition that was presumably issued under Mozart's supervision, contains a large number of dynamic indications,[31] which, because of their profusion or their nature ("crescendo" and "diminuendo", for example), were all but unrealizable on the harpsichord, it seems safe to assume that the work in question was intended for the piano, or just possibly for the clavichord.

*          *

*

Up to about 1770, pianos were still scarce. The piano did not appear on a public concert platform until 1767, and "the world's first piano recital" was given, by J. C. Bach, in London the following year,[32] the same year in which a Paris audience first heard the instrument in a concert hall. [33] There is no evidence that young Mozart, on tour or at home, at any time up to his final return from Italy in 1773, played in public any clavier but the harpsichord. It seems safe to say, therefore, that all the compositions for or with clavier written by him during this period were intended for the harpsichord. This is certainly true of the violin sonatas in this group (K. 6-15, 26-31), all of which were published soon after they were composed; according to the title pages of the first editions they are all "pour le Clavecin . . . avec l'Accompagnement de Violon".

The songs of this period, however, may have been written with the clavichord in mind as much as the harpsichord or spinet, just as those

[29] See Curt Sachs, Sammlung alter Musikinstrumente bei der staatlichen Hochschule für Musik zu Berlin, 1922.

[30] An f-sharp''' appears in the clavier part of the G major violin Sonata, K. 379, as printed in the Gesamtausgabe, but this note is not in the first edition (Vienna, 1781). Similarly with the EE in Mozart's cadenza for the last movement of the clavier Concerto in B-flat, K. 456, which, though in the Gesamtausgabe, is not in the André edition of the cadenzas. The e'''' in the printed score of the four-hand Sonata in G, K. 357, is in a portion of the work that was written by Julius André after Mozart's death. I believe that the f-sharp''' in the last movement of the Sonata in D for two claviers, K. 448, is an editor's insertion. The oldest source I have been able to consult is the Breitkopf & Härtel edition of 1803.

[31] The Gesamtausgabe is quite unreliable in this respect. The frequent use there, for example, of the symbols < and >, and of the term "legato", does not represent Mozart's own practice.

[32] Curt Sachs, "The History of Musical Instruments", 1940, p. 395.

[33] Michel Brenet, Les Concerts en France sous l'ancien régime, 1900, p. 292.

composed later were probably intended as much for the clavichord as for the grand or square piano. Most of the songs with German text were doubtless written for performance in intimate surroundings, and the ubiquity of the clavichord in German households must have been taken into account by Mozart when he wrote them.[34]

The nature of the clavier called for in the works written between the fall of 1773 and November, 1777, is not certain. The compositions in question are two sets of variations (K. 179, 180), the four-hand Sonata in B-flat (K. 358), probably the *canzonetta, Ridente la calma* (K. 152), a Divertimento for clavier, violin, and 'cello (K. 254), an Allegro in G minor (K. 312), six sonatas (K. 279-84), four concertos for clavier and orchestra (K. 175, 238, 246, 271), and the Concerto for three claviers (K. 242).

Except in the case of the six sonatas, there is nothing to show that any of these works were not intended for the harpsichord. The concertos, particularly, from the standpoint of style, seem to call for that instrument. This is true also of a work composed somewhat later — the Concerto for two claviers, K. 365 (1779), which displays no especially pianistic traits; it was apparently intended for use by Wolfgang and his sister in Salzburg, and was consequently very probably planned for harpsichords (*cf.* p. 80). Leopold Mozart actually refers to K. 242 as the *"Clavier Concert a 3 Clavecin".*[35] Some of us may feel that the variations on Salieri's *Mio caro Adone* (K. 180) and the Sonata for four hands (K. 358) sound better on the piano, but this is a matter of opinion.

Concerning the set of six sonatas, however, we are in somewhat better case. They are the first of Mozart's compositions for clavier alone in that form. They were written, in part, according to Einstein in the new "Köchel", for the trip Mozart took to Munich towards the end of 1774. We have seen that Mozart played the piano in Munich that very winter. These works contain dynamic indications, including *"crescendo"* and *"decrescendo"*, in extraordinary profusion, far more than in any previous clavier works by Mozart and more than in most of his subsequent ones. To realize all of these shadings would have been a virtual impossibility on an 18th-century harpsichord. It would seem as though Mozart, knowing that he would encounter pianos in Munich, took advan-

---

[34] *Das Veilchen* and *Das Lied der Trennung* were published in Vienna in 1789 as *"Zwey Deutsche Arien zum Singen beym Clavier"*. Of such "arias" in general, Auerbach writes: "All the odes and songs 'with clavier accompaniment', 'for singing at the clavier' ... are ... to a certain extent 'clavichordistic'; in any case they are always playable on the clavichord." (Auerbach, p. 75.)

[35] Schiedermair, Vol. III, p. 229.

tage of this knowledge to emphasize in these works effects possible only on an instrument like the piano, the nature of such effects being known to him from his familiarity with the clavichord and from such experience with the piano as he may already have had.[36]

By the end of 1777, Mozart, as we have seen, found pianos wherever he went; and the reports of contemporaries,[37] combined with information yielded by the MSS[38] and the internal evidence afforded by the music itself, leave no doubt that all the clavier works written from that time on, with the probable exception of K. 365, must have been intended for the piano. By internal evidence is meant the style that results when a work is planned for the piano, as distinguished from the style of a work planned for the harpsichord. Mozart's maturest piano style, to be sure, contains many elements that started life in answer to the needs of an instrument with plucked strings; but its most characteristic elements are those called into existence by the possibilities afforded by having hammers instead of quills. Thus embellishments, being no longer needed to emphasize particular tones, tend to disappear, the melodic line acquires a more flowing, song-like character, and sustained tones appear more frequently and are used with greater effect.

It was very likely the tone quality of the piano that led Mozart to one of his innovations in the field of orchestration: the skilful blending, in the later concertos, of woodwind and horn tone with the smooth,

[36] In the letter in which he described Stein's pianos Mozart remarked that he had played his six sonatas frequently in Munich and in Mannheim and that "the last one, in D, sounds exquisite on Stein's pianoforte". Wyzewa and Saint-Foix believe that the first five sonatas were definitely intended for the harpsichord and that only the one in D, K. 284, was written for the piano. (*W.-A. Mozart,* Vol. II, p. 215.) But even on the basis of the notes alone, it is difficult to find ground for agreement with these great scholars about the first five sonatas. If the first and last movements of K. 279 are in pure harpsichord style, the Andante is not; and the style of the lovely slow movement of K. 280, which seems like a study for the Adagio of the A major Concerto, K. 488, is not at all apt for the harpsichord but is well suited for the piano or clavichord.

[37] An example: A correspondent in Cramer's *Magazin der Musik* reports from Vienna, under date of March 22, 1783: "Today the celebrated Herr Chevalier Mozart gave a concert for his benefit in the National Theatre . . . The two new concertos and other fantasies that Herr Mozart played on the forte piano won a most enthusiastic reception." (Vol. I, p. 578.) One of the concertos was K. 415 and the other K. 175 with K. 382 as a new finale.

[38] Some examples: The superscription on the autograph MS of K. 457 reads in part: "*Sonata. Per il Pianoforte solo.*" This work was published together with K. 475 in Vienna, 1785, as "*Fantasie et Sonate Pour le Forte-Piano*", one of the very few of Mozart's clavier works published in his lifetime that were not issued "*pour le Clavecin ou Pianoforte*". K. 526, according to the autograph MS, is a "*Sonata per Piano-forte e Violino*"; and the clavier part of the E major trio, K. 542, is marked "*Piano-forte*" in the original MS.

liquid piano tone, a blending impossible to achieve if, instead of piano tone, one of the elements of the mixture had been the comparatively edged, pinched tone of the harpsichord.

The available evidence, then, justifies the assumption that all of Mozart's sonatas for solo clavier, all the clavier concertos beginning with K. 414, and all the chamber music with clavier composed after 1777 were intended for the piano. To believe that a performance of any of these works on a modern grand piano accurately represents what Mozart had in mind, however, is another matter, at least as far as tone quality is concerned. It is important to remember that the Stein, the ideal instrument for Mozart's piano works, differed from modern pianos in several essential respects. Hans Brunner has described a Stein piano and others of its type and has compared them with earlier as well as later instruments. He finds that the pianos of the Stein type, while retaining the agility, the clear-cut tone quality and rhythmic precision of harpsichords and earlier pianos, have in addition the all-important ability to sing. "The chief goal [in the construction of these pianos] is sustained, singing, clear tone, of sufficient volume and carrying power, but thin enough to be clear and elastic."[39] The modern piano, with its much larger dimensions, its iron frame, its longer and thicker strings, its heavier sounding-board, produces tone that is more diffuse, less elastic; and it can be made to sing a melody only with difficulty. Nevertheless it is our opinion that a performance of a Mozart piano work, by an intelligent and sensitive artist, on a modern piano, is closer to what Mozart must have had in mind than a performance on a harpsichord.

[39] For full particulars, see Hans Brunner, *Das Klavierklangideal Mozarts und die Klaviere seiner Zeit,* 1933.

# MOZART AND HAYDN

## By ERNST FRITZ SCHMID

M OZART and Haydn — those two names have generally come to connote a stylistic era traditionally known as "Viennese Classicism." Upon closer investigation, however, it turns out that this neat label is in many ways less than adequate or appropriate. The lives of the two men fill a time-span of considerable length in such a manner that Joseph Haydn's long life of 77 years encloses within its center the brief, extraordinarily concentrated creative life of Wolfgang Amadeus Mozart. We forget much too readily that at more or less the same time when Joseph Haydn was born in the Lower Austrian frontier village of Rohrau, the cantor of St. Thomas's at Leipzig was busy writing his Mass in B minor, that Handel, master of the Italian Baroque opera, was celebrating his greatest triumphs in London, and finally that one of the sopranos of the Augsburg church choir was a 13-year-old boy named Leopold Mozart. The same pompous and solemn world of the Baroque in which Leopold grew up was the environment that Joseph Haydn entered when in 1740 he started his musical career as choir boy at St. Stephen's in Vienna; his young mind received its musical education from the compositions and writings of the great masters of the Viennese Baroque — the aged Johann Joseph Fux and the recently deceased Antonio Caldara.

For Mozart the Baroque traditions were primarily a part of his ancestral heritage rather than an immediate artistic experience, except for the traces of Baroque style that were perpetuated in the Salzburg school-drama and, especially, in church music, which, under the influence of the aged Johann Ernst Eberlin, remained closest to past traditions — a trait that has always been typical of church music. Thus, Mozart's occasional reversion to the Baroque in his later years was due less to such impressions as he might have gathered in his youth than to the strong stimuli he received from Central and North German Baroque music, with some of which he had become acquainted as a result of the antiquarian interests of Gottfried van Swieten. Haydn followed similar stylistic procedures in his later years. But in his case this was primarily a conscious utilization of personal impressions, gained from such Baroque music as the works of Gregor Joseph Werner, with whom he had long been associated as assistant and whom he succeeded as conductor; for Haydn, the manuscripts of Werner's works were among his most prized possessions.

Thus, Haydn and Mozart are not rooted in identical musical traditions. While the former still had some degree of direct contact with the Baroque, that style reaches the young Mozart only indirectly through his father. Wolfgang grew up in the age of *Empfindsamkeit* and of the *style galant,* and his enlightened father acquainted him with a number of fashionable works, as can be seen in his early musical notebooks. Mozart was only ten when he came under the decisive influence of the particularly congenial art of Johann Sebastian Bach's gifted youngest son, whose world was already far removed from that of his father.

However, to say that the little pieces in the study books prepared by Leopold Mozart for his son and pupil were nothing but choice selections of art music in the *style galant* would be to disregard part of the evidence. A careful examination of these books discloses that Mozart was exposed to another sphere — that of native folk music, with which none of the great masters remained unacquainted. And once again we become aware of a process quite similar to that which revealed itself when we compared the relative position of the two masters in the tradition of art music. This becomes quite clear when we consider their respective birthplaces.

It was on his deathbed that Beethoven, while looking at a picture of Haydn's birthplace, is supposed to have made this comment to a friend of his: "You see, dear Hummel, this is the house in which Haydn was born; someone made me a present of this picture today, and I get a childish delight from it. Only a poor peasant's hut, and what a great man was born there!" And it was indeed a pretty wretched place in which the composer of *The Creation* and *The Seasons* was born. His father, a lowly peasant and wheelwright, lived at the edge of the small village on the Leitha River. Young Haydn's environment consisted of the idyllic undulating landscape surrounding Rohrau and the unpretentious God-fearing family life centering around the typical daily chores of a Lower Austrian peasant and craftsman. And Haydn's first musical experiences came exclusively from the sphere of native folk music, which was a part of the daily life of the peasantry. Moreover, his father, while an apprentice, had learned to play the small harp, which frequently was the instrument of journeymen in those days; oftentimes he would play an accompaniment, while Haydn's mother would sing one of the many folksongs of the Leitha district, where her family had lived for generations. The diversity of the folk music of this district was reinforced by foreign influences penetrating the border area. Specifically, it was Croatian and Hungarian folk music that flourished alongside the German variety and was to become so important a factor in Haydn's style.

How different was the environment in which the young Mozart grew up! His father was a highly educated person and respected court musician, whose Swabian native town had throbbed with the bustle of a German commercial center and with a cultural life in which his ancestors had participated for generations. Mozart's mother came from a family of Salzburg officials whose pride, gaiety, and enlightenment were typical of the class and the locale. Hence the type of house in which Mozart was born — an elegant, beautifully appointed middle-class residence in the center of a city whose cultural life had the comfortable atmosphere typical of an 18th-century archiepiscopal court. Salzburg's musical culture centered around its luxurious aristocratic society, and the young boy in his silken, gold-embroidered dress suit, guided by his father, quickly and naturally assimilated the conventions of this society as soon as he began to participate in concerts. Effortlessly he entered a world to which the little peasant boy from Rohrau gained admission only after his tenacious struggle as a starving student in Vienna.

In the small circle of a Salzburg middle-class family and especially in the home of Leopold Mozart folk music was heard only in the somewhat stylized *art form,* no matter how simple, of humorous songs and entertaining clavier pieces. In this category belong the merry little pieces that Leopold Mozart wrote into Wolfgang's music books. Most of those guild songs, Swabian dances, and trumpet pieces were very probably reminiscences from the father's student days of songs and the music current among the students in the Benedictine monasteries of Swabia and Bavaria. This environment of the young Leopold Mozart was the same with which Valentin Rathgeber, the merry monk of Banz, had been familiar; the latter's *Ohrenvergnügendes und gemütsergötzendes Tafelkonfekt*, a delightful collection of popular monastic music, a belated offspring of the medieval *Carmina Burana*, had appeared right during Leopold's student years in Augsburg, published by the Augsburg house of Lotter, later the older Mozart's own chief publisher. It has been proved repeatedly that Wolfgang occasionally used melodies preserved in the *Tafelkonfekt*, in the Swabian *Ostracher Liederhandschrift*, and in similar sources.

It is only natural that Joseph Haydn, in view of his direct contact with folk music, would have come under its influence to a much greater extent than Mozart. Numerous works of his, from any period of his life, utilize material from the folk music he had been exposed to during his youth. The fact that in his home district German and foreign cultural traits persisted side by side often lends a special charm to his music; again and again we encounter not only German folk tunes, but also Croatian, Hungarian, and Gypsy material (a circumstance that has led several scholars to erroneous conclusions regarding Haydn's nationality). Moreover, Haydn, by dint of these early stimuli, gradually became a veritable musical folklorist, who collected folk music wherever he found it, and immortalized it in his works when he deemed such a procedure suitable. This accounts for his melodies from French chansons or those based on Scottish and Russian folksongs, etc. It is noteworthy that folk-musical influences manifest themselves particularly in his greatest and most ambitious works such as the London symphonies, while Mozart as a rule relegates them to more modest compositions, especially the relatively playful cassations and divertimentos.

Even the physiognomy of the two masters strikingly reveals the basic difference of their character as determined by family background, general environment, and education. Pictures of Haydn show the face of a man who comes from true peasant stock, deliberate, kindly, and bright; his eyes reveal a well-adjusted mind capable of calm judgment. Like the plants of his native province he matured slowly, as did Anton Bruckner, his later brother from Upper Austria, whom he also resembles in several other ways. Like Bruckner, Haydn was in his forties when he wrote his first mature works, compared with which his many earlier compositions, however numerous and charming, seem like preparatory efforts. In fact, most of the works that are well known these days come from Haydn's later years; and for our purposes it is well to remember that those particular works were written after Mozart's death. This is true of such oratorios as the *Seven Words* (cantata version), the six great Masses, the mature symphonies (e.g. the *Drumroll, Clock,* and the *Military)*, many of his late string quartets *(Horseman, Fifths, Emperor),* and a number of other compositions. —"Haydn always wears peasant stockings," said a Viennese Haydn enthusiast recently. This astute comment is true not only of his music, in which the healthy, matutinal freshness of the folk music of his native Leitha district comes to the fore so frequently, but also of his purely human qualities. Slowly and deliberately, but with purposeful tenacity, he mastered the difficulties of his early life; the ground covered by his development would in the case of other families have required the effort of generations. He had to acquire his extensive education autodidactically and only gradually gained access to the society that had accepted Mozart since his youth. Through careful management of his household affairs — every evening up to his last years he had his servants submit the day's bills to him for his approval — he even accumulated a considerable fortune.

Mozart's portraits betray a totally different personality — a sensitive person whose intellectual heritage was the product of generations of cultural refinement. His eyes alone reveal his vivacious, impressionable, and uncommonly quick mind, so different from Haydn's deliberate, patient nature. It is easy to see that the genius speaking to us from these eyes had matured early. In almost breathless haste he spent his short life on his art; a constant drive urged him on. Hardly more than a boy, he created works that to this day are the objects of wonder. His whole creative life was one vernal tempest, a ceaseless response to his divinely inspired artistic tasks. When Mozart's life was completed, Haydn, who survived him by almost twenty years, had just reached the peak of his creativity.

The courtly atmosphere of the archiepiscopal city of Salzurg and of imperial Vienna, in which he grew up and spent most of his life, has left its traces in Mozart's works. His minuets — artistic sublimations of courtly dance music — reflect a world that is completely different from Haydn's. The typical minuets of Mozart's mature period with their elegant sensitivity and exquisite dynamics, rhythms, and harmonies contrast strikingly with the peasant rhythms of Haydn's minuets, many of whose trios, particularly, are reminiscent of the ultimate origin of this music; often they seem to conjure up a picture of the hearty and vigorous scene offered by Lower Austrian peasantry stomping about to the tune of a *Ländler*.

And so we find ourselves confronted with the question to what extent it is possible to demonstrate personal and artistic contact and mutual influences in the life and works of the two composers. Much has been written about this topic, more still has been copied and repeated, and it will be worth while to separate the chaff from the wheat.

At the time of Mozart's birth, the 24-year-old Haydn had already written his first string quartet. That same year his beloved entered a Viennese convent, and Haydn wrote a melancholy organ concerto in memory of his first love. It is a strange coincidence that, just like Mozart some decades later, he wound up with the sister of his beloved, although the dire consequences far exceeded Mozart's lot. His wife, the bigoted, nagging, and slow-witted daughter of a Viennese wigmaker, for whom he on occasion used "bestia infernale" as a special term of endearment, made life miserable for him. (A special irony of fate caused both men to send their wives on frequent vacations to the same resort town, beautiful Baden, near Vienna. In fact, Mrs. Haydn might be said to have established her vidual headquarters in that place while her husband was still alive. Lacking physical attractiveness, she was, of course, unable to have as good a time as Constanze Mozart.)

After the misery of his Viennese student years Haydn finally found security when, in 1761, he joined the musical establishment at the Esterházy court in Eisenstadt, beginning as assistant conductor. At this time, the five-year-old Mozart was composing his first little pieces. Two years later the proud father paraded the unprecedented miracle of his son's musical genius before Viennese aristocratic society. It is unlikely, however, that the two musicians met at that time, or for that matter, on the occasion of the Mozarts' second visit to Vienna in 1768, since Haydn's court service kept him in Eisenstadt or still farther away at the prince's country estate in Eszterháza near the Neusiedler Lake.

But even though opportunities for Haydn to visit Vienna were rare indeed, the works of both composers from that time begin to show some remarkable instances of mutual influence. In the finale of a symphony, dated 1763 in the manuscript, Haydn uses the well-known four-tone motif that has justly been called Mozart's "Leitmotiv"; it has become most famous because of the finale of the *Jupiter Symphony*. Haydn contrasts the theme with a number of different counterpoints, profiles it by means of varying instrumentation, including the solemn sonority of the horns, and even introduces a four-part stretto, which strikingly resembles the stretto of the same theme in the Credo of Mozart's F-major Mass of 1774. Not that this Credo is the first occasion on which Mozart utilizes his favorite motif; strangely enough it already appears, especially emphasized by the horns, in the slow movement of his first symphony, which the eight-year-old prodigy wrote in London near the beginning of 1765. Since Haydn's symphony — No. 13 in the Breitkopf *Gesamtausgabe* — had been composed a short time before, in 1763, and since, moreover, Haydn's works were at that time especially popular in Paris, where as early as January and March 1764 La Chevadière and Venier for the first time published some of his compositions (six string quartets and a symphony), it is a not altogether unreasonable assumption that the young Mozart may have seen a copy of this symphony during his stay in Paris in 1764. (It so happened that in January 1764 some of Mozart's compositions also appeared in print for the first time, and in the same place as Haydn's; these were the sonatas for piano and violin, dedicated to Princess Victoire of France.) Another point of contact between the two masters may have been Haydn's brother Michael, who a little earlier, in 1762, had been appointed conductor of the Salzburg court orchestra and in this capacity undoubtedly familiarized local circles with a number of his brother's works.

It is, of course, a well-known fact that Mozart often used the above-mentioned motif; we find it in the Sanctus of the C-major Mass of 1776, in the B-flat major Symphony of 1779, in the E-flat major Violin Sonata (1785) and finally, transfigured through the artistry of Mozart's maturity, in the *Jupiter Symphony*.

A similar strange instance of mutual influence between Haydn and the young Mozart is contained in Mozart's sprightly *Galimathias musicum*, which he wrote in March 1766 at The Hague on the occasion of the investiture of William V of Orange. At one point in this orchestral suite, a quodlibet arrangement of a number of folk tunes, the horns and oboes play the rather rugged Alpine folksong of the *Eight Sow-Tailors*. Towards the end of the piece there appears over a fermata the word "Capriccio," which probably means, in accordance with the original sense of the word (goat's leap), a riotously gay improvisation. Haydn uses the same tune in a piano composition entitled *Capriccio Acht Sau-*

*schneider müssen sein.* The autograph is dated 1765, antedating Mozart's *Galimathias* by one year. (Haydn revised the piece in 1789 when he published it.) It is, of course, perfectly true that the tune itself may have been the immediate stimulus for both composers. But the temporal closeness of the two compositions is striking, and it is not at all unreasonable to assume that Mozart, perhaps again through Michael Haydn, the jovial friend of the Mozart family, had had a chance to see a copy of Haydn's piece before he wrote his *Galimathias.*

We can take it for granted that by 1770 a number of Joseph Haydn's works were well known to the Mozarts. This is indicated by a letter written by Leopold to his wife in August 1771. Father Mozart, who was at the time visiting Verona with his son, asks in this letter for some music intended for a friend of his in Milan: "So, let Nannerl look for the two trios, one by Joseph Haydn in F with violin and 'cello, and the other in C; it says 'Wagenseil' on it." Which Haydn trio is meant here is not certain; presumably it is the one numbered 27 in the Peters edition, an early work in three movements, in which he introduces a very original passage in instrumental recitative style after the manner of Carl Philipp Emanuel Bach, a composer equally admired by both Haydn and Mozart. In view of Mozart's early acquaintance with some of Haydn's many clavier trios it remains puzzling that he himself did not write his first work for this particular instrumental combination until August 1776.

Mozart's string quartets, however, reveal that in this field Haydn's influence was already considerable in the early seventies. This was doubtless due to Mozart's stay in Vienna in 1773, where Haydn's fame was now beginning to grow, while, strangely enough, only French and English amateurs and publishers had paid any attention to his works up to that time. Haydn's "Sun" quartets, Op. 20, written in 1772, are of especial importance for Mozart's development. (The name was inspired by a vignette of the rising sun on the title-page of an edition brought out by the Berlin publisher Hummel in 1780.) In these quartets Haydn, probably under the influence of Gregor Josef Werner, his predecessor in Eisenstadt, reverted to Baroque procedures. The finales of three of the six quartets are extended, learned fugues, written in the manner of Werner's quartet fugues, which Haydn owned and published as late as 1805 "because of my special esteem for this celebrated master." These quartets of Haydn are in general distinguished from their predecessors by artful contrapuntal workmanship and by the seriousness of the composer's approach to form and content. Especially noteworthy is the fact that, as a result of this contrapuntal attitude, Haydn deprives the first violin of its erstwhile almost unlimited leadership.

Musical circles must have been quite impressed by these novel quartets. Only one year later, Florian Gassmann, a talented composer whose family was on friendly terms with Haydn, wrote string quartets with extensive fugal finales. And Mozart, who was in Vienna in 1773, likewise was influenced by Haydn's quartets; his six Viennese quartets of that year are distinguished by a wholly new tone and sound, a result of contrapuntal texture. Mozart further follows Haydn in that for the first time he includes the minuet as third movement. The only earlier quartet of Mozart's — his first — originally consisted of only three movements; the fourth was added in 1773. The *Andante* of the first of Mozart's Viennese quartets offers the most striking specific example of relationship to Haydn's "Sun" quartets. In this movement — as well as later in the Kyrie of his Requiem — the composer uses a well-known Baroque theme, made famous by Handel in his *Messiah* ("And with his stripes we are healed"). The same theme had been utilized by Haydn in the fugal finale of Op. 20, No. 5; even the key is the same in both cases. A comparison of the two movements is instructive, especially in view of our previous comparison of Haydn's thirteenth with Mozart's first symphony. Just as he had done with the Mozart motif in his early symphony, Haydn uses the "Handel theme" in a lively *allabreve* movement, treating it contrapuntally in the artful tradition of Gregor Josef Werner. Mozart, on the other hand, assigns the same theme the function of a main theme for a slow movement of deeply expressive character, a musical thought-process quite similar to that which we had noticed in the slow movement of his first symphony.

Beginning with the 1770's there is increasing evidence of Haydn's influence on Mozart; sometimes it is immediately apparent in the latter's thematic invention, but more often in the development of his compositional technique. During the same decade Haydn, searching for greater formal unification and intensification, progressed from severe contrapuntal work to a freer though well-integrated part-writing. This process, resulting in the victory of thematic development, shows itself first in the symphonies of the 1770's; the nature of many of the themes already suggests their suitability for the motivic work of the development sections with their variegated instrumentation. Mozart knew these symphonies well. On the reverse of one of the Mozart autographs from the early 1780's — a piano cadenza — we find that the composer jotted down the themes of three of the most important Haydn symphonies of that time (Nos. 47, 62, and 75). And these three symphonies are especially significant for the musical relationship between Haydn and Mozart. That the second movement of No. 62 (1777), an *Andante* in 6/8 meter with muted strings, is in form and content highly reminiscent of the letter duet from Mozart's *Figaro* was already pointed out by Carl Ferdinand Pohl, the venerable dean of Haydn research, even though he was unaware of the abovementioned external evidence. Karl Geiringer, who likewise had no knowledge of the abovementioned Mozart manuscript, noticed nonetheless that the main theme of Haydn's symphony No. 75, composed prior to 1782, demonstrates how successfully Haydn in turn assimilated the highly subjective style of his younger colleague and friend. And indeed, we have here the first case of the older master's coming under Mozart's influence, a process that becomes more noticeable later on. At this time, however, the reverse relationship still prevails.

The early 1780's witness the closest contact between the two masters. After Mozart had gathered a wealth of experience and artistic impressions on his trip to Mannheim and Paris, he found himself again in the service of the hated Archbishop of Salzburg. The famous incident between Mozart and his two superiors — Colloredo and his chamberlain, Count Arco — caused Mozart to sever his relations with the Salzburg court and to embark on the life of an independent artist in Vienna. For Haydn, too, continuing in his activity as princely court composer and conductor, there were undoubtedly occasions on which he must have lost his patience and wished to exchange his Hungarian exile for an independent life in the imperial city, capital of empire and music alike. But Haydn, whose personality was so different from Mozart's, could not possibly be pictured in the kind of situation that caused Mozart's break with the Salzburg court. His attitude towards the feudalistic absolutism of his time was conditioned by the patriarchal orientation of his peasant forebears, most of whom had spent their lives as humble vassals of the Counts Harrach. Even when he was well on in years he was not much troubled by his status as a higher type of court servant; and in spite of the wealth, honor, and social standing that came to him in the wake of his triumphs in England, he used to say: "I have associated with emperors, kings, and many great lords, and they have told me many flattering things. But I wouldn't want to become familiar with such people; I prefer to associate with people of my own class." This attitude sets him apart from Mozart, the son of an enlightened middle-class family, a genius who from his boyhood had always had access to the highest social strata, who proudly asserted that only the heart could confer true nobility, and who, fully aware of his intellectual superiority, passionately resisted all social restriction. And so society — the same society that never tired of celebrating the old Haydn — abandoned Mozart to a pitiful fate.

Mozart's first great success in Vienna came in 1782 with the performance of *Die Entführung aus dem Serail*. Seven years earlier Haydn had composed his *opera buffa, L'incontro improviso,* in Eszterháza; both operas were based on essentially the same Turkish subject that eighteen years before had served Gluck for his *La Rencontre imprévue*. Although there is no proof, it may well be that word about Haydn's opera had reached Vienna and that Mozart and Stephanie derived some of their ideas from it.

On the whole, the field of opera provided the two composers with few points of contact, even though Haydn, who in 1790 had moved to Vienna, displayed a lively interest in Mozart's work on his *Così fan tutte* and attended the rehearsals with him. His own operatic output ended in 1784 with the Italian "dramma eroico" *Armida,* written for Esterházy's theater; later on, in London, he began work on the *Orfeo* theme, but this remained a fragment, which, incidentally, is more reminiscent of Gluck than of Mozart. After Mozart's *Figaro* (1786), which impressed Haydn to such a degree that the opera haunted his dreams even after his return to Eszterháza, he gallantly and with full conviction abandoned the field of opera to Mozart. This is borne out by the splendid letter he wrote to a Prague music-lover after the première of *Don Giovanni* in October 1787:

> You ask me for an *opera buffa*. With pleasure, if you feel like having a specimen of my vocal composition all to yourself. But if you want to have it performed, I can't be of service to you, because all my operas are too closely bound up with our personnel at Eszterhaz in Hungary; elsewhere they would thus never have the effect I calculated for this place. It would be a different story, of course, if I had the inestimable good fortune to compose an entirely new libretto especially for the Prague theater. But this, too, would be a risky business, since hardly anyone could expect to be the equal of the great Mozart ...If I could only impress the inimitable works of Mozart on the souls of all music-lovers and especially of the great men of this world and with the same deep musical understanding and the same great emotion with which my soul receives them: the nations would vie for the possession of such a jewel. Prague should not only hold on to that wonderful man, but reward him; the history of unrewarded geniuses is sad and gives posterity little encouragement

for continued striving; which is why unfortunately so many promising minds lie prostrate. I am indignant that this *unique Mozart* has not yet been appointed to an imperial or royal court! Forgive me for digressing, but I love that man too much.

These words reflect the deep impression Mozart's artistic personality had made on Haydn since they first met in the 1780's. For a short period each winter Prince Esterházy used to come to Vienna, bringing his orchestra with him, and this custom undoubtedly provided the first opportunity for a personal meeting of the two composers. It is odd that, as far as we know, so great a patron of music as Esterházy never seized the opportunity to establish some sort of relationship with Mozart. Even Beethoven was some years later invited to perform his C-major Mass before another prince in Eisenstadt; but we know nothing of Mozart's ever having stayed at the Esterházy court. It may be that the prince was influenced by the aging Empress Maria Theresa's negative attitude towards the Mozarts.

Although we do not know for certain just exactly where in Vienna the two composers met for the first time, it may be assumed that this happened in one of the distinguished middle-class homes where their music was admired and frequently performed. One name that deserves special mention is that of court counselor Franz Bernhard Ritter von Kees, the patron of the famous concerts in the Augarten, in which Mozart so often performed. It was in his house that most of the symphonies Haydn wrote in the 1780's, i.e. especially the so-called Paris symphonies such as the still well-known *La Reine, L'Ours,* and *La Poule,* were rehearsed before they were presented to a broader public; the master of the house participated as violist or 'cellist, and oftentimes the composer himself was present. The semiweekly private concerts in Kees's residence were attended by the foremost Viennese artists, among them Haydn, Dittersdorf, Albrechtsberger, and, according to the young Gyrowetz, Mozart, who would frequently play the piano and write songs for the lady of the house. (A catalogue of all the Haydn symphonies owned by Kees was found by Jens Peter Larsen in the princely music archives of Thurn and Taxis at Regensburg and has been published by him in facsimile.)

Another house in which, according to the memoirs of the Austrian poetess Karoline von Pichler, Haydn and Mozart, as well as Paisiello, Cimarosa, and Salieri, were frequent guests, was that of her father, court counselor Franz von Greiner, who belonged to the same Masonic lodge that Haydn joined in 1785. Here again we find a common bond between Haydn and Mozart, who had become a Freemason some months earlier. Some doubt remains whether Mozart visited the home of the famous physician Peter Leopold von Genzinger in the Schottenhof, whose wife Marianne was warmly admired by Haydn. We do know, however, that Marianne, who was an accomplished pianist, performed many a Mozart work for Haydn. In 1789, isolated in Eisenstadt, Haydn wrote her a letter that contains the following remark: "Well, in God's name this, too, will pass and the time will come when I shall again have the inestimable pleasure of sitting next to you at the piano, hearing Mozart's masterworks performed, and kissing your hands in gratitude for all those beautiful pieces!"

Mozart must have known Frau von Genzinger, since Haydn in his letters from London would occasionally ask her to deliver a message to Mozart. Haydn's correspondence with her contains numerous passages revealing his friendly admiration for and cordial confidence in his younger friend. At one point, having been informed by both his wife and von Kees that Mozart was rumored to have made deprecatory remarks about him during his absence, he writes: "However, I can't believe that Mozart should have disparaged me. I forgive him. That here in London I also have to put up with a good bit of professional jealousy is certainly true; I know almost all the persons involved, mostly Italians." Thus Haydn and Mozart both faced the same hostility from the Italian camp, and if Mozart ever made a remark that malicious persons might have interpreted as directed against Haydn, it could only have been in reference to the older master's skill in the ordinary affairs of life; Mozart, of course, completely lacked Haydn's ability to make his artistic successes pay.

In addition to the homes of the Kees, Greiner, and Genzinger families there was another residence where Haydn and Mozart used to meet in the mid-eighties, socially as well as to perform music together. In this case it was an artist who arranged the parties, the English composer Stephen Storace, who was renowned as a composer of comic operas; he lived in Vienna with his sister Nancy, the first Susanna in Mozart's *Figaro*. The Irish singer Michael Kelly tells of having attended a chamber-music soirée at Storace's house, during which quartets were performed by the following select personnel: 1st violin — Haydn; 2nd violin — Ditters von Dittersdorf, who was visiting Vienna; viola — Mozart; and 'cello — the Bohemian composer Johann Baptist Vanhal. Among the audience at this musicale, whose program undoubtedly included works by the performers, we find again Paisiello, whom Mozart admired greatly, and the Italian poet Abbate Casti.

The warm friendship between Haydn and Mozart, which was the result of such meetings, gave the impetus for one of Mozart's most glorious works, the quartet cycle of the years 1782-85, which he dedicated to Haydn. Sometime in January 1785 he produced the six quartets in his own home "for his dear friend Haydn and other good friends." When soon after this occasion Mozart's father came to Vienna to witness his son's successes in person, a part of this program was repeated in Mozart's house. Leopold reports the event to his daughter in characteristically graphic fashion:

> On Saturday evening we had Mr. Joseph Haydn and the two barons Tindi with us, the new quartets were played, but only the three new ones which he added to the other three we have — they are a bit lighter, but excellently put together. Mr. Haydn said to me, "I say to you as an honest man before God, your son is the greatest composer I know personally or by name; he has taste and, moreover, the greatest knowledge of composition."

With reference to his son's elegantly furnished apartment on the second floor of the stately house in the Schulerstrasse he says: "That your brother has a beautiful home with all appropriate furnishings you may conclude from the fact that he pays a rent of 460 gulden." Considering how many Mozart houses no longer exist, it is a fortunate accident that this house was preserved, the house in which he wrote *Figaro* and in which that memorable encounter of the two composers took place that cemented their noble friendship for all time.

No matter how bold and willful these string quartets may be, it is apparent that in many ways Mozart used as models the so-called Russian Quartets, Op. 33, which Haydn had written a few years earlier. In these quartets, written nine years after the "Sun" quartets and dedicated to Grand Duke Paul of Russia, Haydn applied the same technique of thematic development that he had already begun to introduce into his symphonies. Mozart carried this new trend to unprecedented heights in the "Haydn" quartets, in which the pre-Beethovenian string quartet reached a peak unsurpassed even in later times. Mozart himself considered Haydn's work above all as the conceptual basis for his quartet style, as is borne out by his remark, "I have learned from Haydn how to write quartets." (When Leopold Kozeluch, a minor Viennese composer, on whom many years later Beethoven bestowed the honorary title "Miserabilis," dared to criticize Haydn's quartets in his presence,

Mozart put him in his place with the following outburst: "Sir, even if the two of us were fused together, we wouldn't make a second Haydn by a long shot!") The well-known Italian dedication with which he prefaced these six quartets demonstrates his reverence for his model, no matter how conscious he was of his own achievement.

This warm, ungrudging friendship endured till Mozart's death; in fact, Haydn never ceased to honor Mozart's memory. They both shared the intensive experience of Baroque music to which they had been introduced by a mutual friend, the odd, patriarchal music-lover Gottfried van Swieten. Some of the results of these stimuli were the mighty fragment of Mozart's C-minor Mass and Haydn's imposing *St. Cecilia Mass,* products of the same artistic spirit and equal high points in the creative careers of the two composers.

It is strange that by the 1780's Haydn had just about forsaken the field of the piano concerto, while Mozart was just then producing his masterpieces in that genre, so different from Haydn's earlier, unpretentious concertos. In 1784 Haydn wrote his last work in this field, the D-major Concerto with the well-known *Ongarese* finale, even though in those years he must have had a number of opportunities to hear Mozart's latest creations in this genre. We must assume that, in view of Mozart's extraordinary achievements, Haydn's modesty once again, as in the operatic field, caused him to renounce competition with the younger composer.

In 1788, when Mozart wrote his last three magnificent works in symphonic form, Haydn, having just finished his Paris symphonies, was working on the *Oxford Symphony,* which he later resuscitated for the ceremonies in England when he received his honorary doctorate. His last twelve symphonies, which contain many an instance of assimilation of Mozartean traits, were written after Mozart's death, as were also the greatest of his string quartets, oratorios, and Masses. Thus, Haydn offers one of the rather infrequent examples of an artist who, having been model and inspiration for a younger genius, in his mature years is himself creatively enriched by the works of this younger master.

At the time of Mozart's final illness Haydn had reached the pinnacle of his fame. Daily he was showered with invitations and festivities by his enthusiastic English admirers, including such dignitaries as the Prince of Wales and the Lord Mayor of London. Under the circumstances he was totally unaware of his friend's tragic plight. When in December 1790 Haydn departed from Vienna, Mozart had

49301

expressed his presentiment of events to come by saying, "I fear, my father, that this is our last farewell." However, he was not so much worried about himself as fearful about the hazards of a trip to a strange country, especially for a man nearly sixty years of age. Mozart had himself insistently tried to dissuade Haydn from the trip. The possibility that he might precede his older friend in death seemed quite remote to him. The fact is that the London impresario Salomon had invited him as well as Haydn to go to England, but despite the economic prospects he could not make up his mind to accept, and promised to go after Haydn's return to Vienna. He did not live to see again the friend who was one of the few contemporaries to appreciate his genius and to understand him as an artist.

Haydn was deeply shaken by the news of Mozart's death, as is evidenced by a passage from his letter to Frau von Genzinger: "I'm looking forward with a childish pleasure to getting home and embracing all my good friends; I only regret to be unable to greet the great Mozart this way, if indeed it is true that he has died, which I hope not to be the case. Not for a hundred years will posterity see such a talent." Early in January 1792 he wrote the following words to Johann Michael von Puchberg, the Viennese merchant who had been Mozart's most faithful and helpful friend during his last desperate days:

For some time I was completely beside myself at the news of his death and simply couldn't believe that an irreplaceable man like him should be fated to leave this world so soon; I only regret that his death prevented him from convincing the still uninformed Englishmen of what I've been preaching daily . . . Will you, my dear friend, please be good enough to send me a list of the pieces that are not yet known here. I shall try my best to promote them here for the benefit of his widow; I had written the poor soul only three weeks ago, that I would devote all my strength and ability to giving free composition lessons to her favorite son [the 8-year-old Karl Thomas], as soon as he is old enough, so as to replace the father at least to a certain extent.

When the London music publisher Broderip asked him whether he should purchase the manuscripts of the deceased master, which the widow had offered him, he answered: "By all means, buy them. He was truly a great musician. My friends often flatter me about my talent; but he was far above me."

In the years after Mozart's death Haydn, at the peak of his creative powers, never forgot Mozart. This is borne out by a statement reported to us by his friend, the Italian poet and biographer Giuseppe

Carpani, who asserts that in his seventies Haydn still insisted that he had never heard a work by Mozart without having learned something from it. And indeed we encounter numerous Mozartean reminiscences in the master's late works, such as the bass motif in the *Qui tollis* of his *Nelson Mass,* which seems directly inspired by the *Tuba mirum* of Mozart's Requiem. Of greater significance are certain more general stylistic features indicative of Mozart's influence, such as Haydn's refined use of the winds and his inheritance of Mozart's masterful technique of individualization of instrumental sonorities. On the whole, the instances revealing influences of the younger man on the older one are less notable than those reflecting the reverse situation. Haydn's late style, which strongly influenced the young and middle Beethoven, differs considerably from Mozart's and is essentially autogenous.

Of the many utterances from Haydn's last years that indicate his continuing attachment to Mozart and his work the following sample especially deserves to be quoted: "Mozart's violin quartets and the Requiem alone suffice to make him immortal, even if he had written nothing else." When the 77-year-old master died in the spring of 1809 no worthier work could have been performed during the public memorial service than this very Requiem by his friend, whose death had preceded his by so many years. The fact that a copy of the relief portrait of Mozart made by the sculptor Leonhard Posch in 1788 was discovered beside the scores of *Don Giovanni* and the Requiem among Haydn's effects testifies to the fond remembrance he retained for his friend. It was this friendship of two great artists — one of the most beautiful instances of such a friendship in the history of art — that Franz Niemtschek had in mind when he wrote the dedication to his Mozart biography of 1798: "This small tribute to the immortal Mozart is herewith dedicated with the greatest admiration to Joseph Haydn, father of the noble art of music and favorite of the Graces."

*(Translated by Ernest Sanders)*

# REQUIEM BUT NO PEACE

## By FRIEDRICH BLUME

I N 1825 Gottfried Weber, in his periodical *Cäcilia,* began that famous, indeed notorious, attack on the authenticity of Mozart's Requiem which initiated a controversy that has lasted now for almost a century and a half. The first to reply was Mozart's old friend, Maximilian Stadler, with his *Verteidigung der Echtheit (Defense of the Authenticity),* to which he added two supplementary articles in the same year, 1826. Weber lived in Mannheim and had never seen the autograph manuscripts of sections of the Requiem. His attack was based partly on stylistic considerations, partly on his Romantic-Classicistic conception of the nature of church music, and partly on reports that he had received from Anton André in Offenbach. The completed portions of the autograph (Introit and Kyrie) are said not to have "turned up" until 1838, a year before Weber's death (a statement that has long been recognized as inaccurate). Stadler, on the other hand, lived in Vienna, was a personal friend of Mozart's, helped Konstanze during her widowhood, called himself a friend of G. von Nissen, had close relations with the court Kapellmeister J. L. Eybler, and must have known well Mozart's pupil and amanuensis, F. X. Süssmayr. For a time he himself had possessed parts of the autograph, which he later presented to the Vienna Hofbibliothek; he had made several copies of the whole work, had completed the figures for the bass in Süssmayr's copy and in copies of the score published by Breitkopf & Härtel (1800), had collated the autograph portions with the Breitkopf edition and in at least two copies had entered the letters M. and S. to indicate Mozart's and Süssmayr's contributions. Moreover, he had marked in pencil Eybler's contributions in the autograph, and where Mozart's handwriting resumes after Eybler, added a "Moz." That he had a better insight than Weber into the working out of the composition and its posthumous history is obvious. It must be said for Weber that he had made careful inquiries (see the accounts in Jahn and Abert), but his information was only second- or third-hand. His most important authority, André, had already drawn partly mistaken conclusions from the investigation he had instituted in Vienna, and refused to budge from them. Stadler writes of him (to Konstanze April 3, 1826): "I know Herr André too well, and know how obstinately he sticks to his preconceived opinions." Weber himself was prejudiced, and grew more and more bitter in the course of the controversy. Stadler was eight years older than Mozart and outlived him by a long time: he did not die until 1833. Eybler, nine years younger than Mozart, died in 1846, Konstanze Mozart in 1842. Only the one state's witness, who could have given the most accurate testimony (if he wanted to), Süssmayr, died before his time, in 1803.

Since 1825/26 the conflict has not subsided. The "question of authenticity" has been debated innumerable times from every conceivable point of view, using the memoirs of those concerned, letters and reports of contemporaries, investigations of the sources, and stylistic and esthetic arguments, and the heroes of the battle have pulled every imaginable stop, from academic *noblesse* to Homeric insult. There is complete agreement on only one point, and on that point Weber, Stadler, and André had already agreed: that it would never be possible to clear up completely all the doubts and questions raised by the Requiem. It would seem that it is precisely the awareness of this point that has caused the conflict constantly to flare up again, down to the present time: attempts are made to gain new aspects from the sources and to unite with the old findings new ones that turn up, sparsely enough, here and there. The result, however, is that the problem as a whole today seems more confused than ever.

Actually, "the" problem of the Requiem has for a long time now divided itself into three problems, which are, to be sure, pigeonholed together, but which should be kept separate, insofar as they can be, for an orderly investigation. They are

1) the authenticity problem in the narrower sense,
2) the instrumentation problem,
3) the dating problem.

The authenticity problem in the narrower sense lies in the question of which parts of the composition are by Mozart himself, which were carried out by him more or less extensively and completed by another hand, and which were composed on the basis of Mozart's outlines or sketches or perhaps altogether freely invented. The instrumentation problem concerns the question to what extent Süssmayr's manuscript of the Sequence, the Offertory, the Sanctus (with Benedictus), the Agnus, and the Communion, which Count Walsegg possessed, and Süssmayr's corresponding copy of it, which was used to engrave from by Breitkopf & Härtel for their first edition of the score (Konstanze got it back from them and later presented it to Stadler), represent Mozart's specifications for instrumentation or come from more detailed, but now lost, elaborations by the master, or whether (except for the few rubrics by Mozart) only Süssmayr's hand is to be discerned in the instrumentation of these movements. The dating problem must still of necessity concern itself with the question whether the work before us, insofar as it is by Mozart, is really the Requiem of the last months of his life, the work, surrounded by myths, that he undertook on commission from Count Walsegg in July 1791 and that still occupied him on his deathbed and over which death snatched the pen out of his hand, or whether the fragment that survives in Mozart's hand does not perhaps belong to an earlier period of his activity, whether he did not complete larger portions of the work than we know about today before the journey to Prague for the première of *Tito* (at which event Mozart was already severely ill) — that is, from July to August 1791, and stopped work on it before that journey.

It is certainly not useless to say that none of these questions has been satisfactorily answered up to now. The present status of the controversy may perhaps be best understood if we proceed from Einstein's summary.[1] Einstein postulates, so to speak as an axiom, an assertion that is not proved, not provable, and indeed unlikely: that other than the

---

[1] *Köchel,* 3rd ed., Ann Arbor, 1947, p. 808 ff.

well-known fragmentary autograph of the Vienna Nationalbibliothek,[2] "exactly" nothing exists in Mozart's hand. This assertion contradicts the statement, constantly repeated by all contemporary and immediately following witnesses, that Süssmayr had received from Konstanze Mozart in addition to the autograph score a quantity of "Zettel" (slips of paper) — therefore no doubt sketches and outlines —, a statement that Vincent Novello,[3] too, confirms on the basis of conversations with Konstanze, Eybler, and Stadler.[4] Einstein's assertion also contradicts the sense of Süssmayr's own statement that Mozart had "often played and sung through with him the pieces that had been set to music" and "very often spoke to him about the completion of this work." The latter cannot refer to the completed but only to the uncompleted portions of the work, and such instructions and conferences could surely not have taken place without something in writing as a basis. Einstein's assertion contradicts, too, the sense of Konstanze's numerous remarks according to which Süssmayr received formal instructions from Mozart, and her letter to Stadler of May 31, 1827,[5] in which she writes: "Even if we assumed that Süssmayr found fragments by Mozart, the Requiem would still be only Mozart's work." The quantity of statements to the effect that sketches by Mozart existed is overwhelming. Former investigators, however, attached no particular significance to them because those writers proceeded on the assumption that Mozart seldom worked from sketches. But more recent research has shown in increasing measure that Mozart certainly used sketches and outlines, and indeed apparently more than ever towards the end of his life. Einstein's thesis does not stand up under close examination. The contrary is probable.

His assumption made, the further course of events appeared quite simple to Einstein. Süssmayr copied the unfinished portions, completed them as best he could, composed what was missing, and then delivered

---

[2] Vienna, Nationalbibliothek MS 17561 a-b. Facsimile ed. by A. Schnerich, Vienna, 1913. It should perhaps be pointed out that Schnerich's edition comprises only the predominantly autograph portions of the MSS a and b. Introit and Kyrie (old pagination fols. 1-10) are taken from MS a; the other portions, insofar as they are present in Mozart's handwriting, constitute MS b (old pagination fols. 11-45). Süssmayr's copy and contributions from the Sequence to the end comprise the second part of MS a (new pagination fols. 11-64); they are not included in the Schnerich edition.

[3] *A Mozart Pilgrimage,* ed. by N. Medici and R. Hughes, London, 1955, p. 119 ff.

[4] In the literature the communication appeared first in I. von Mosel, *Über die Originalpartitur des Requiems von Mozart,* Vienna, 1839.

[5] Stadler's second supplement.

to Count Walsegg the whole thing, "the first two movements in Mozart's original, the others in Süssmayr's handwriting, which is deceptively similar to Mozart's." Only "with the reappearance of the manuscript (1838)" did comparison with Süssmayr's manuscript lead "to the true state of affairs." It will be demonstrated below that this sentence contains two fundamental errors.

Einstein's position in the dispute about authenticity may be summed up in his own brief formulation: "The controversy . . . would have been unnecessary if people had wanted to believe the explanation that Süssmayr had delivered to Breitkopf & Härtel . . . on February 8, 1800 (and which was continually questioned ever since André's 'Preface' of 1826)."[6] Truly, an astonishing statement for a historian, especially for one as skeptical as Einstein otherwise was. "Believe the testimony of the man who plays the cloudiest and most disputed role, and the controversy vanishes" — an all too easy solution. If Süssmayr's explanation was so completely trustworthy as Einstein would have us believe, it would not have been questioned by others in addition to André, like Novello (1829), and implicitly F. S. Silverstolpe as early as 1801, and even closer to the scene, Konstanze, Eybler, and Stadler.

Einstein quietly ignored two essential points of view. The first is the following: Süssmayr states in his explanation of 1800 that Mozart finished the vocal parts and the figured bass of the "Requiem with Kyrie" "but of the instrumentation only indicated what was to be done [das Motivum] here and there." This is in direct contradiction to the actual situation, as is shown by the autograph and as Schnerich also recognized. The Requiem and Kyrie movements are complete in Mozart's handwriting, although they may have been written not in one stretch but at two different times. Süssmayr therefore claimed credit here to which he was not entitled. Since the autograph of the Introit and Kyrie was then in Count Walsegg's possession, Süssmayr may have assumed that the discrepancy would not be noticed. To be sure, he must have known that Stadler had made a copy before the work was delivered; in 1828 Stadler presented it, together with the autograph fragments that had been in his possession since 1827, to the Vienna Hofbibliothek.[7]

[6] This explanation is reprinted complete in Einstein, p. 810, and elsewhere.

[7] *Pilgrimage*, p. 124. Presented — not sold, as the inscription on MS 17561b implies (Schnerich, p. 11). — D. Kerner, *Ist das Requiem Mozarts Schwanengesang?*, in *Schweizerische Musikzeitung*, C (1960), 70-75, believes (p. 72) that Süssmayr also claimed for himself the *Domine* and *Hostias* sections of the Offertory, but there is no mention of this in the latter's explanation.

The discrepancy should have struck Einstein the more forcibly because it was precisely this that had already led André astray.[8] On the basis of Süssmayr's statement, André thought that Mozart could only have made a "draft" of the Introit and Kyrie also, and he therefore felt justified later in transforming the two movements into a sketch according to his own ideas.[9]

Stadler's copies, on which this last score edition of André's was based, are today the property of the Stadt- und Universitätbibliothek of Frankfurt am Main.[10] The copy of the *Dies irae* (that is, the whole Sequence up to and including the *Confutatis*) is completely faithful to the original down to page and measure and even the random traits of Mozart's handwriting, and bears the superscription: "Abbé Stadlers Abschrift des Mozartschen Manuskripts, welche er mir am 21. August 28 in Wien verehrte. André" ("Abbé Stadler's copy of the Mozartean manuscript, which he presented to me in Vienna August 21, 1828. André"). Even the foliation 11-32 matches the original. Eybler's entries are of course lacking, since this is only a copy of Mozart's autograph. With respect to the delimitation of Mozart's and Eybler's contributions (Eybler's writing is in fact extremely like Mozart's, while the same cannot be said of the samples of Süssmayr's handwriting that Schnerich reproduced), Stadler departed in details from his earlier pencil draft, for example in the *Dies irae* measure 5, in the *Tuba mirum* mm. 44-53 and again 54 to the end,

[8] *W. A. Mozarti Missa pro defunctis Requiem . . . Partitur. Neue, nach Mozarts und Süssmayrs Handschriften berichtigte Ausgabe. Nebst einem Vorbericht von Anton André . . .,* Offenbach, Johann André, Pl. No. 5018. The *Vorbericht* (Preface) is dated Dec. . 31, 1826 — that is, before the copies of the autograph portions, made for him by Stadler, were in his hands. The edition appeared in 1827.

[9] *Partitur des Dies irae, Tuba mirum, Rex tremendae, Recordare, Confutatis, Lacrymosa, Domine Jesu und Hostias von W. A. Mozarts Requiem, so wie solche Mozart eigenhändig geschrieben und Abbé Stadler kopiert hat,* Pl. No. 5246, published in 1829. This edition, to which too little attention has been paid, is an engraved facsimile, as it were, of the autograph portions of the score, following Stadler's copies of 1828 (see below) page for page and sheet for sheet so exactly that even the blank pages are reproduced. The edition is a fine indication of how conscientious André was about investigating and making known the true state of affairs. The same publisher who had brought out a piano-vocal score as early as 1800 and a full score in 1827 turns with this edition to Mozart's "friends and admirers" in order to settle the dispute. The fact that, being then still in ignorance about the autograph Requiem and Kyrie, he sketched those movements in an arbitrary way, according to his notion of how Mozart must have left them, does not lessen the value of the edition. The not unimportant foreword is dated May 1829.

[10] Mus. Hs. 211. I am greatly indebted to Dr. W. Schmieder for calling them to my attention and making them available to me.

in the *Recordare* mm. 107-08, and so on. Although in the original manuscript he had specifically marked the basset horns in mm. 26-29 of the *Confutatis* "Moz.," in 1828 he did not include them in his copy. It is plain that in details even Stadler was already not always sure whose handwriting was before him. The copy of the *Lacrimosa* and the Offertory, written on separate sheets,[11] does not follow the original pagination exactly; but the original foliation is entered occasionally at the appropriate measure. This copy seems to have been prepared at another time and is not dated. The superscription reads: "Gegenwärtige Abschrift des betreffenden Theiles von Mozart's Requiem ist Note um Note, Blatt um Blatt, ganz genau nach dem Mozartschen Manuscript durch meinen verehrten Freund, Herrn Abbé Stadler, für mich gefertigt worden. André." ("The present copy of the corresponding parts of Mozart's Requiem was made for me exactly according to Mozart's manuscript, note for note, page for page, by my honored friend Abbé Stadler. André.") Once more Stadler followed the autograph strictly; the *Lacrimosa* consequently lacks the two soprano measures, "huic ergo parce Deus," added by another (Eybler's?) hand. The copy ends with the words "Quam olim da capo." The first part comprises, with the movements from *Dies irae* to *Confutatis,* that portion of the autograph which was then in Stadler's own possession; the second part, with the *Lacrimosa* and the Offertory, the portion owned by Eybler, which had been presented to him by Konstanze.

One sees what far-reaching consequences followed from Süssmayr's incorrect statement, and one understands the restraint disclosed by Stadler, Eybler, and Konstanze concerning the work of one who had died years before. No publisher took such pains to ascertain the truth as André. Quite in contrast to Einstein one comes to the conclusion that the dispute could indeed have been settled long ago, not, however, by taking Süssmayr's explanation at face value but by checking it. André tried to do so but was led off on a false trail. Those most closely concerned were fully aware of the true state of affairs; the only thing they did not know was to what extent Süssmayr possessed Mozartean material in addition to the autograph portions that have come down to us.

The second point of view that Einstein ignored is the following. From Süssmayr's day to our own, strong doubts have been expressed that he was capable of composing the completion of the *Lacrimosa* and the

[11] Kept under the same call-number.

wholly missing movements as they were done. At least the *Lacrimosa,*[12] the Benedictus, and the Agnus reveal the hand of a master of Mozart's rank — who could it have been, if not Mozart himself? Vincent Novello, who had an especially good knowledge of the church music of his time,[13] noted in his travel diary that there was nothing by Süssmayr that could justify the assumption that he was capable of composing the missing sections. He goes so far as to suggest that Mozart composed, in essentials, the Sanctus, Benedictus, Agnus, and *Dona* even *before* the (composed but not orchestrated) Offertory; these sections were then turned over to Süssmayr merely for "remplissage" (which Süssmayr used to supply for Mozart occasionally, for example for *Tito*), and only then did Mozart begin work on the Offertory. Süssmayr would then have destroyed the fragments that had been given him. While this is all mere conjecture, it is undoubtedly based on the conversations Novello had with Konstanze, Eybler, and Stadler. It gains in significance by fitting very well with the results of Schnerich's investigations. According to Schnerich, Mozart's work proceeded in three stages. In the first (which Schnerich dates from July to August), Mozart composed the Introit, the Kyrie fugue to measure 29, and the Sequence up to and including the *Rex tremendae,* working out the instrumentation of these sections, however, only in the preludes and interludes. The second stage (which Schnerich dates as late as October, consequently after the trip to Prague) saw the completion of the Kyrie fugue, the continuation of the Sequence up to and including the *Confutatis,* and the beginning of the Offertory *Domine Jesu;* Mozart also finished the instrumentation of the Introit and the Kyrie. This was followed by another interruption, caused by Mozart's illness (he was bedridden from November 20, 1791, on) and the composition of the cantata K. 623, after which the composition of the *Domine Jesu* was continued, the composition of the *Hostias* begun and finished, and at the very end Mozart began the *Lacrimosa.* Since Schnerich concluded that the movements were composed not in the order of their succession in the text but unsystematically and that the Offertory came into existence before the *Lacrimosa,* the possibility arises that Mozart composed other sections too, like the Sanctus or the Agnus, before portions that precede them in the text, or at least prepared outlines

[12] W. Fischer, *Das Lacrimosa dies illa,* in *Mozart-Jahrbuch 1951,* pp. 9-21, prefers another solution of the *Lacrimosa* but is also convinced that the "slips of paper" handed over to Süssmayr contained sketches by Mozart for this movement, and conjectures (p. 12) which measures they may have concerned.

[13] See especially the travel notes gathered together in the last part of the *Pilgrimage.*

for them. Why would Mozart have had such long conversations with Süssmayr, why would he have given him such detailed instructions, if not about such outlines? Certainly not about the movements that were completely composed, and certainly not about questions of instrumentation alone. Those conversations *may,* however, have dealt only with movements that had been more or less extensively composed and with instructions for their "remplissage." That is why Konstanze had said repeatedly that Süssmayr had only done "what anyone could have done." Evidently F. S. Silverstolpe[14] was echoing the opinion shared by Stadler, Eybler, and Konstanze when he wrote in 1801 that the four numbers "in which the Master's own pen cannot be recognized" (that is, Sanctus, Benedictus, Agnus, and Communion) were, "if they are not merely fair copies of rough drafts that Mozart had destroyed (possibly because of many changes made in them), worked out either from outlines made by the Master himself or from instructions by him." Silverstolpe's copy of the score in Stockholm specifies (according to Mörner) quite definitely that the *Lacrimosa* and the *Domine Jesu* are exclusively by Mozart and "completely worked out" by him.

How Einstein arrived at his *jurare in verba magistri* Süssmayr remains hard to understand. His idea was that Konstanze, in her dealings with Breitkopf & Härtel, must have felt obliged to make Mozart's share appear as great, and Süssmayr's as small, as possible; and that if then, contrary to this interest, Süssmayr represented his share as so important, credence must be given him. That this motive imputed to Konstanze could not have been decisive is already clear from the fact that in her correspondence with André,[15] she did not once consider it worth mentioning the Offertory with verse (*Domine* and *Hostias*), which her husband had composed. In her letter of June 2, 1802, to Breitkopf & Härtel[16] Konstanze expresses her surprise that Süssmayr, although obliged to return only Mozart's autograph portions, after finishing his work also gave her the Sanctus, "in which not a note or a word is in Mozart's handwriting"; she would have liked an explanation and had inquired of Süssmayr but had received no information. Does not this indicate that Süssmayr looked upon the Sanctus too as essentially a product of Mo-

---

[14] C.-G. Stellan Mörner, *F. S. Silverstolpes im Jahr 1800 (oder 1801) in Wien niedergeschriebene Bemerkungen zu Mozarts Requiem,* in *Festschrift Alfred Orel,* Vienna, 1960, pp. 113-19.

[15] E. Anderson, *The Letters of Mozart and His Family,* London, 1938; Vol. III contains a selection from Konstanze's letters to André, ed. by C. B. Oldman.

[16] According to Abert (1921), II, App. XIII, p. 1020 f.

zart? As early a writer as A. B. Marx had attempted[17] to attribute to
Mozart those movements claimed by Süssmayr. If Einstein, therefore,
had not already stumbled over Süssmayr's misleading report on the
"Requiem with Kyrie," the stylistically and qualitatively unequivocal
state of affairs, in agreement with the views of contemporaries, should
have led him at least to a more cautious judgment.

With respect to "the authenticity problem in the narrower sense,"
it is evident from all these considerations that the matter is by no means
as simple as Einstein would have it. The assumption operative up to now,
according to which Süssmayr is to be considered the composer of the
missing portions as long as nothing can be proved to the contrary, seems
today less justified than the assumption that the independent composition
of the closing portions cannot be ascribed to Süssmayr so long as the
doubts concerning his talent, doubts expressed again and again from all
sides since 1800, are not resolved by demonstrating a corresponding
accomplishment of his own from his pen. As long as no church compositions by Süssmayr can be brought forward that at least imitate faithfully the master's style (as J. G. Goldberg, say, was capable of doing
in relation to J. S. Bach),[18] it is in fact irresponsible to attribute the later
movements of the Requiem to the unproved pupil as his own compositions. No such evidence, however, has appeared. Up to now, no investigation of Süssmayr's surviving church compositions has been undertaken.
But as long as no evidence of that kind is produced to the contrary, we
must continue to hold with Novello (and others) that Süssmayr
possessed extensive outlines by Mozart, which he merely carried out and
which he then — whether inadvertently or deliberately — destroyed.
C. F. Pohl already thought that Süssmayr had destroyed many sketches,
and believed (quite in accordance with the contemporary evidence)
that much more in the Requiem stemmed from Mozart, or at least
represented his exact intentions, than was known.[19] Süssmayr ought not
on that account to be accused of "fraud" or "forgery,"[20] and to throw
away carelessly a quantity of sheets of sketches by Mozart could hardly
have seemed to him like sacrilege. Süssmayr was a modest and certainly
an indigent musician who preened himself a little on borrowed plumage,

[17] *Berliner musikalische Zeitung,* 1825, p. 371 f. (according to Jahn).

[18] Cf. *Das Erbe Deutscher Musik,* Bd. 35, ed. by A. Dürr, 1957.

[19] *Grove,* 5th ed. (1954), VIII, 193.

[20] C.-A. Moberg, *Äkthetsfragor i Mozarts Rekviem,* in *Acta Universitatis Up-
saliensis,* 1960:4, pp. 71, 75.

but he was no genius, nor was he a genius-imitator. At least, there is no evidence whatever that he was.

The history of the autograph, too, as told by Einstein is not entirely free of error or not quite complete.[21] Stadler left his portion of the autograph (the Sequence except for the *Lacrimosa*), which he had acquired from an unknown person, to the Hofbibliothek not in 1831 but in 1828 or 1829, as Novello reports.[22] That the autograph of the Introit and Kyrie was "missing"[23] from 1791, that is, from the time of delivery to Count Walsegg, to 1838, that is, to its purchase for the Hofbibliothek through Count Dietrichstein, is not correct according to Silverstolpe's communications[24] and André's preface of 1826. The whereabouts of this autograph seems to have been unknown in 1800; according to Silverstolpe, Konstanze published an announcement in the press in order to find it. Its owner at once made it available to her, in the house of his lawyer, *Advokat* Sortschen, Unter den Tuchlauben, Vienna, for the purpose of collating it with the Breitkopf edition of the score. The collation was made by Stadler in the presence of Eybler and Silverstolpe and the results entered in Konstanze's and Silverstolpe's printed copies, both copies being marked with the letters "M" and "S." Silverstolpe's is in Stockholm; Konstanze sent hers to André on January 26, 1801, together with the autograph — at that time still in her possession — of the Sequence up to and including the *Confutatis* (the same that Stadler acquired in 1827 from the unknown person). For the collation were available the Introit and the Kyrie from Walsegg, the first five movements of the Sequence owned by Konstanze, and the *Lacrimosa* and *Domine Jesu,* all in Mozart's autographs, as Silverstolpe expressly confirms — consequently everything that is autograph contained today in the MS 17561 a-b of the Nationalbibliothek in Vienna. At that time Eybler possessed the *Lacrimosa* and the Offertory; Novello saw them at Eybler's still in 1829; these pieces did not go to the Hofbibliothek only at his death (1846) but were already there in 1838 or 1839. At the collating, the repetition of the *Quam olim* and of the *Te decet* with the Kyrie fugue in the Communion were present in Süssmayr's handwriting, as were the Sanctus with Benedictus, the beginning of the Agnus, and, remarkably enough, the first seven pages of the *Hostias* too. Also noteworthy is the

[21] P. 808.
[22] *Pilgrimage,* p. 124.
[23] Einstein, p. 809 f.
[24] Mörner, p. 113 ff.

fact that Silverstolpe records the first five movements of the Sequence as "in Mozart's and Süssmayr's mixed handwriting"; it is to be assumed that Silverstolpe regarded Eybler's entries in Mozart's autograph as Süssmayr's. The most remarkable thing about this collating, however, is the fact that the still living cause of all the doubts, and the only person who could have resolved them, was not invited. Süssmayr lived in Vienna, and nothing can show the distrust the participants had for him more clearly than the fact that they did without him on this unique occasion.

Be that as it may, it is certain that the autograph was in no way "missing." The *Lacrimosa* and the Offertory were presented to Eybler by Konstanze. The first five movements of the Sequence passed from her through a still unknown hand to Stadler in 1827, and Stadler had seen and collated in 1800 the autograph of the Introit and Kyrie in Walsegg's possession. It is therefore all the more strange when Stadler, in a letter to Konstanze of April 3, 1826,[25] writes, after he had just surprisingly acquired the first five movements of the Sequence: "There is now lacking for Mozart's complete manuscript of this work nothing except the first movement: Requiem and Kyrie" and when he expresses the same thought again in a further letter to Konstanze of March 14, 1827. Contradictorily enough, however, Stadler writes in his *Defense of the Authenticity* in the same year, 1826: "thus I could set down here definitely the name of the owner." Stadler can hardly have forgotten that he had held this autograph in his hand in 1800, and if the lawyer at that time was perhaps not authorized to disclose the name of the owner, Stadler makes it plain now that he knows it. Konstanze, too, in her letter to André of November 26, 1800,[26] speaks of a "secret"; she knows that "the anonymous one has in the original everything that precedes the *Dies irae*." Did she really not know the name then, or was she only pretending ignorance?

It does not matter. What is important is that no part of the autograph was ever completely missing and that those most closely concerned were acquainted with the situation all along. But now Einstein's basic statement, that only "at the reappearance of the manuscript (1838)" comparison with Süssmayr's manuscript led "to the true state of affairs," collapses: the manuscript did not reappear only in 1838; what was in

---

[25] E. H. Müller von Asow, *Ungedruckte Briefe zum Streit um das Requiem,* in *Wiener Figaro,* XI (1941), 2 ff.

[26] André, Preface, 1826.

Count Walsegg's possession was made available and known as early as 1800, and what was not in his possession was between 1800 and 1838 in the hands of Konstanze, Eybler, and Stadler — consequently in no way "missing" — and the "true state of affairs" did not come to light only after 1838 but was known to all those immediately concerned and even to visitors to Vienna like Silverstolpe and Novello. Only outsiders like André and Weber, who received their information third-hand, were partly deceived about the situation. At the same time the "authenticity problem in the narrower sense," in contrast to Einstein's attempt at simplification, is once more unfolded in all its complexity, from which only the one conclusion can be drawn, namely that until the contrary is proved, not Süssmayr but Mozart must be considered in essentials the composer of the Sanctus with *Pleni*, Benedictus, and *Osanna* as well as the Agnus and that Süssmayr did nothing more than the "remplissage," as Novello calls it, or as Konstanze says, "what anyone could have done."[27]

Compared to the questions concerning the "authenticity problem in the narrower sense," the "instrumentation problem" has been treated like a stepchild in the literature up to now, even though this is not only the weakest spot in the tradition of the Requiem,[28] but this question is of first importance in performance and for the understanding of Mozart's wishes. No account is usually taken of how sparse the original indications are. Aside from the two violins and violas, which are of course indicated everywhere ('cellos, double basses, and bassoons, when they do not have obbligato passages, customarily play along with the organ bass), Mozart wrote only the following indications:

> for the Introit and Kyrie: two basset horns, two
> bassoons, two trumpets, timpani;
> for the *Tuba mirum:* trombone solo (up to m. 18);
> for the *Recordare:* two basset horns.

That is all. Before the *Confutatis* is the inscription: two basset horns, two trumpets, and timpani; it seems very doubtful, however, that this is in Mozart's hand, especially since the notes following the inscription

---

[27] This view was already expressed in 1932 in the Foreword to my edition of the Requiem score for Eulenburg: but at that time I still honored the older view, that Mozart usually did not work from sketches. Since then I have learned better. Not even the article by C.-A. Moberg mentioned in Note 20 has been able to weaken this view by sound arguments.

[28] I called attention to this in 1932 in the preface to my edition (see Note 27) and recently in my article *Mozart* in *MGG,* IX, col. 788.

are unquestionably not in his hand and were quite correctly encircled in pencil by Stadler — consequently they come from Eybler — while Mozart in no other place wrote down the name of an instrument without at least sketching (as in the *Recordare,* for example) the first notes of the part in question. In other words, in the autograph only the Introit and Kyrie have that instrumentation which today covers the whole work like a thick, gray crust, comparable to the layer of whitewash that was plastered over the naves of Gothic churches in the period of restoration. If the combination in these two movements, unusual as it is for Mozart, is to be taken as intended to be final at all, then it represents a particular color-conception that Mozart prescribed for this place. There is however no basis for the opinion, occasionally expressed,[29] that this instrumentation was intended by Mozart for the whole Requiem. The sources say nothing about it, and not a single one of Mozart's other large church works displays such uniformity. The nearest to it chronologically, the C minor Mass of 1783, offers on the contrary a picture of the greatest variety of color. The same is true of Haydn's late Masses. Here, in the Requiem, another, unMozartean conception of the nature of church music was at work, a soberer, more rational, more joyless one. The tendency of the classicistically inclined waning century to regard as noble innocence and calm absence of passion in late Mozart what is in reality passion compressed and turned inward, the tendency that preferred *Tito* to all other operas of Mozart, finds here its church-music reflection.

That the original yields so little is not strange. Mozart's working habit in compositions with orchestra was to write down in a first draft whatever voice was leading at the moment (perhaps the solo instrument or the vocal part) and the bass and to fill in the pauses in the main voices by interludes of an instrument, perhaps the first violin; not until a second time round did he add the orchestration, and very often it was only in a third time round that he extended and completed the writing for the wind groups, as may be seen in many symphonies, concertos, and so on. Wind supplements are often not even entered in the score itself but the additional wind parts follow the score in individual parts or in a small score. Whether, therefore, the instrumentation of the first two movements should be regarded as completed cannot be definitely determined. For the other movements the condition of the autograph and the number of staves provided yield no conclusion concerning the

[29] For example by C.-A. Moberg (see Note 20), p. 74.

orchestration that Mozart imagined. What faces us from the beginning of the Sequence on is nothing other than what he would normally have written down at a first draft, even if not pressed for speed or harassed by illness. Only Introit and Kyrie show the second stage of work (as Schnerich, too, has demonstrated). Since trumpets and drums are already entered, it may perhaps be assumed that a further addition of winds in a third stage of work was not contemplated. Nevertheless there remains for consideration the fact that the orchestration of Mozart's church works is never to be regarded as final; the city archives of Augsburg contain parts, supplied by Leopold or Wolfgang Mozart and bearing autograph insertions or corrections by Wolfgang, formerly owned by the Holy Cross monastery, for movements for example of the Masses K. 262, 257, 258, 275 but also for the Litany K. 195 whose instrumentation exceeds the indications given in Köchel-Einstein. Mozart's true intentions, therefore, remain uncertain. Only one thing may be said with some certainty: the way Süssmayr did it was surely not Mozart's intention. It would contradict all experience.

The unusual combination of basset horns with bassoons, trumpets, and drums in the first two movements permits only two explanations: either Mozart chose them deliberately as "local color," to emphasize the dark character of the first movements, in which case they could not have been intended for the whole work; or Mozart perhaps planned to lighten them by afterwards adding winds, in which case it must be assumed that a colorful instrumentation of the later parts was intended. That flutes, oboes, clarinets, and horns are wholly absent in the complete Requiem is entirely unMozartean and must weaken Süssmayr's credit as much as does his use of the basset horns throughout. This instrument, which was with the clarinet definitely a favorite of Mozart's and which appears in immediate temporal proximity with the Requiem in *Tito* and *Zauberflöte* among other works, was nevertheless always used by him very cautiously and economically. In the first act of *Zauberflöte* it does not appear until the highly dramatic Pamina-Sarastro recitative in the finale, in the second it is heard in the march of the priests, in the "dreimaliger Akkord," and in Sarastro's aria with chorus, after which it vanishes completely from the score for the rest of the opera; that is, it serves only for tone-color characterization of certain persons and situations. In *Tito* Mozart calls for a solo basset horn only once, in the rondo of Vitellia. An especially fine example of the use of the instrument is offered by the *Maurerische Trauermusik*, K. 477, with three basset horns, of which the two top ones were added later.[30] In extensive works Mozart never used the basset horn throughout, except for the special case of the *Gran Partita* K. 361 for twelve wind instruments and double bass. There is nothing to indicate that he planned the uniformity of an instrumentation with basset horns throughout in an extensive church work like the Requiem.

In any case instrumentation cannot have been among the subjects concerning which Mozart is supposed to have instructed his amanuensis so urgently, and if the investigation of the authenticity problem leads to the conclusion that in all probability there is much more in the *composition* that stems from Mozart than has frequently been assumed, as far as the *instrumentation* is concerned we must conclude that of the sound image as Mozart may have imagined it nothing survived for posterity aside from the first two movements (and it is not at all certain that it did for these), indeed that the sources give us no inkling of how the work was meant to sound. Comparison with the *Kunst der Fuge* comes to mind; if Bach had ever intended to perform that work he would certainly not have orchestrated it colorlessly for mere string orchestra, as it is usually performed today.

Some details are worthy of mention. Süssmayr's strengthening of the three lowest voices of the chorus with *colla parte* trombones almost throughout reflects the customary practice of the period in church works; that Mozart too wanted it that way is apparent from the trombone entry prescribed in measure 7 of the Introit in the autograph.[31] Otherwise, whether the trombones should double or not is less a question of tone-

[30] Einstein's supposition (p. 601) that the two upper basset horn parts were composed as "substitutes for the horns" seems to me purely arbitrary. The writing for the basset horns differs too strongly from that for the horns to justify such an assumption, even though they are sometimes in unison with them. We are surely dealing here with nothing other than Mozart's customary procedure, of composing additional instrumental parts in a later stage of work, and this procedure by no means excludes the possibility that he had these instruments in mind from the beginning.

[31] When I edited the score for Eulenburg in 1932 I was not yet aware that this practice was very general in the 18th century. Where the trombones are *colle parti* I did not think it necessary to enter them on separate staves in the score; instead, I simply listed, on pp. IX-X, the few places where they departed from mere doubling. At that time I did not consider the remark "Tromboni" in m. 7 of the Introit to be in Mozart's hand. Today I am of a different opinion, and it would not require a detective (Moberg, p. 70) to convince me of it. But when Moberg accuses me of having falsified the text in this place, he obviously overlooks the fact that I did give the trombone entry on p. IX.

color than of choral technique. Only the *Confutatis,* the Offertory (without the verse), and the Benedictus have obbligato trombones; then there is the controversial trombone solo in the *Tuba mirum.* For the rest, the distribution of the *colla parte* trombones is by no means clear: at the repetition of the *Te decet* and the Kyrie fugue in the Communion the trombones are lacking; they are again notated in the *Osanna II* but missing in the otherwise wholly identical *Osanna I.* The problem here is not one of orchestration but of the current performance practice of the church music of the time, which one conductor would handle in one way and another conductor in another.

The solo trombone with which the *Tuba mirum* begins reaches in Mozart's handwriting up to measure 18, that is for as long as the text speaks of the trumps of the Last Judgment calling the dead to the judgment seat. This is meaningful, and there is no evidence that Mozart wanted to carry it farther. What Süssmayr added in measures 24-34 is superfluous and paltry to boot, the writing in measures 27-28 is technically poor, and the ending, measures 33-34, abrupt. Moreover, misunderstandings have become attached to the solo trombone. André, in his 1827 score, reproduces it as a bassoon from measures 5 to 34, but himself remarks in the Preface that this is very likely an error. In the Breitkopf score the part is printed as trombone, but the Silverstolpe copy also is marked "Fagotto solo" from measure 5 on.[32] Konstanze shows her complete ignorance in matters of instrumentation when in her letter to Breitkopf & Härtel of June 2, 1802, she goes so far as to affirm that in the *Tuba* there is "a certain place where the trombone, not flutes, was intended"; apparently she did not know that there is no flute in the entire Requiem.

Süssmayr's instrumentation teems with thoughtless and gross procedures. The manner in which he can think of nothing better than the tiresome movement of the strings in eighths and syncopations in measures 18 to 40 of the *Tuba,* for example, despite the dramatic accents in the vocal parts, is characteristic (he had certainly taken it over from Eybler, who was also not very inventive); life comes into the orchestra only from measure 40 on — but here it is Mozart's hand, not Süssmayr's, that notated the two violins (the first only in part). A thoughtless vulgarization is evident in the *Rex tremendae.* Here Mozart himself wrote out the whole first-violin part, indicating rests from the second quarter of measure 20 to the end of measure 21 and then notated the final measure

[32] Mörner, p. 119.

again; in measure 21 one can read even in the facsimile the whole rest that originally stood there. In other words, Mozart wanted to have the final prayer of the chorus "Salva me, fons pietatis," which suddenly falls back into *piano,* performed without orchestra. This should not have been overlooked. But Eybler and Süssmayr overlooked it, and in their coarse way orchestrated the rests away. In the *Recordare* Mozart had written out the opening measures for the basset horns and the following string introduction up to measure 14. The basset horns carry out the opening motif of the chorus. What could have been more natural than to let the strings rest at the entrance of the chorus and have the basset horns go along with its upper voices? Instead, Süssmayr has the strings continue uninterruptedly. Only from measure 27 does he employ the basset horns again, this time merely for supporting, and it is only when the chorus resumes the principal motif at the words "Preces meae" that it suddenly occurs to him to have the basset horns go along now — a wholly unMozartean inconsistency. The fact that he took over all these faults from Eybler is little excuse for him. Other passages like these can be pointed out. They should prove that Mozart did not leave workings out of the instrumentation and that he did not give Süssmayr detailed instructions for completing this aspect of the work. In default of any other source we must accept the fact that the "opus summum viri summi," as J. A. Hiller called it on his own handwritten copy, came down to us only as a vocal "res facta," but that its instrumental investiture is irretrievably lost and corrupted.

Finally the dating problem, too, is still not satisfactorily solved. The family tradition and the later account by the singer Benedikt Schack[33] yield the familiar picture: Mozart working on the Requiem up to the last day of his life, the friends assembled around his sickbed and singing every day what had been completed, after his death confusion and the unfinished work turned over to Eybler, then to Süssmayr. Schnerich's theory of stages (see above, p. 110) fits this picture at every point; even the division among the months of the year 1791 assumed by him could be accepted. If the memory of those concerned did not deceive them, the *Lacrimosa* too was sung; it therefore must have been available in finished and written form.

To this tradition, however, objections have been posed all along. Weber believed that the authentic Requiem composed by Mozart was completely lost and that what became known under that title was in reality a composition by Süssmayr based on Mozartean outlines. André thought that the Requiem up to far into the Sequence was an old composition of Mozart's which must have been written before 1784 (before the beginning of the autograph thematic catalogue), perhaps originally to another text, and that he then reworked it into the Requiem, as he did the C minor. Mass into the oratorio *Davidde penitente*. The Offertory, too, if it was by Mozart at all, would be an older work, and in the Sequence André considered the style of late Mozart to begin only at the entry of the "mors stupebit" in the *Tuba mirum*. André defended his views emphatically and stubbornly, and it is not surprising that the aged Stadler became uncertain and wrote in his letter of April 3, 1826, to Konstanze: "A few years ago he [André] visited me and declared that the whole Requiem was written by Mozart long before his death. He did not work on it again shortly before his death. Can this be true? . . . If so, then I have certainly said things here and there in my article [his *Defense of the Authenticity*] that do not agree with such a view. But I was not privy to the secrets of Herr André and wrote frankly what I was thoroughly convinced was the truth after hearing it many times . . ." Stadler too, therefore, knew of the origin of the Requiem in the last months of Mozart's life only through hearsay. In itself, André's argument was quite plausible: Mozart had composed nothing at all for the Church (except the *Ave verum*) since the C minor Mass of 1783, Count Walsegg's commission was not important enough to him (and no doubt not well enough paid) for him to take much trouble with it, he had therefore simply dug up an older work and arranged it or had Süssmayr arrange part of it. André does not believe at all in the mysterious story about the gray messenger and goes so far as to suspect a confusion with an order from King Friedrich Wilhelm II of Prussia, who as early as March 1792 requested a copy of the Requiem.

André's views have recently been revived in a study by D. Kerner,[34] but his arguments have not been given any new foundation. To go so far as André and Kerner would mean nothing less than to accuse the survivors, especially Konstanze, Eybler, and Süssmayr, of a monstrous deception,[35] and Kerner does not hesitate to suggest such a conclusion. The fact is, and this should be clearly understood, that the historical

---

[34] D. Kerner (see Note 7).

[35] Something similar was once undertaken by W. Watson, *An Astounding Forgery*, in *Music and Letters*, VIII (1927), 61-72. The many mistakes, wrong judgments, and inadequacies of this article were corrected at that time on the spot by C. B. Oldman.

tradition of Mozart's work on the Requiem rests on very weak support. Since he did not enter the work after it was begun in his thematic catalogue, although at other times (as André had already pointed out) he occasionally entered "unfinished" works too (that is, compositions that had not yet gone through all the work-stages), it was natural to suppose that the parody or arrangement of an older work could be involved here. Mozart did not enter the parodied portion of *Davidde penitente* in his catalogue either, only the newly composed arias Nos. 6 and 8. But the state of the autograph speaks unequivocally against such an assumption. If Mozart had wanted to parody an older work into a Requiem, he would surely not have copied the score again in his own hand, and in no case would he have done the first two movements in two separate stages and left the later ones unfinished. Also the sketchy condition of the fragmentary instrumental parts in the Sequence and in the Offertory, the corrections in written passages (like the famous crossed-out measure after 29 of the Kyrie fugue), erasures (like *Quam olim*, measure 14), and so on, and especially the way in which notes and text flow entirely out of a single stroke of the pen make the notions of an autograph copy of an older score and the later entering of a new text seem absurd. Surely Mozart would never have spent time on such work, he would obviously have had it done by a copyist. No autograph exists of *Davidde penitente* either. Finally, which work written before 1784 could it have been that found a new use here? An older Requiem or another usable church work would have been mentioned somewhere in the correspondence or at least be known from fragments. In view of these pieces of evidence to the contrary, the André-Kerner hypothesis must be regarded as wholly imaginary.

The autograph definitely comes from Mozart's last period; the handwriting traits and the sketchy manner of working show this, as does the style of the composition. Whether Mozart worked on it up to his final days, as the tradition has it, is another matter. The Italian letter (allegedly to da Ponte) of September 1791[36] cannot be adduced either pro or con; its authenticity is doubtful, and the original has not been available for decades.[37] There are no other remarks in the letters of the last months that could refer to the Requiem. An entry in the autograph thematic catalogue is lacking. The only documentary evidence of the time of origin is the macabre date 1792 over the beginning of the score.

---

[36] Kerner, p. 75.
[37] Information kindly supplied by Dr. O. E. Deutsch in Vienna.

There is not the slightest reason to question the authenticity of this entry ("di me W. A. Mozart mpr. $\overline{792}$"), as Kerner does; it corresponds in every respect with the other writing on the first page of the score and with Mozart's other handwriting habits. To be sure, what it says, and how Mozart came to predate the work so far ahead, must remain undecided. Here every attempt at explanation breaks down.

Too little attention has perhaps been paid in the literature to the letter written by J. Zawrzel, oboist at the Opera in Amsterdam, to André on July 25, 1826, a letter that may nevertheless serve (this is said with all circumspection) to throw some light in the darkness surrounding the history of the origin of the Requiem.[38] André himself tells in his Preface that he sought out this man, who was formerly a musician in the service of Count Walsegg, in Amsterdam in 1825, and that the latter had informed him of the course of events which he then presented once more in his letter. According to this, Zawrzel in August 1791[39] had looked over the Requiem up to the Sanctus in a clean copy on the Count's desk (perhaps in the writing of the Count, who wished to give the work out as his own); he still remembers that he was struck by the basset horns, that he called attention to the fact that it would not be possible to get hold of these instruments in Wiener Neustadt (the town where the Requiem was to be performed), and that he received the reply that the Count would have them brought from Vienna for the performance. This fits with the letter directed by the lawyer Krüchten from Pest on January 3, 1826, to G. Weber,[40] in which it is stated that Mozart traveled to Prague for the coronation of the Emperor (performance of *Tito* September 6, 1791) *after* the performance of the Requiem brought about by the Count in Wiener Neustadt in September 1791. Zawrzel, who stayed on in Vienna in October, continues that after the trip to Prague Mozart thought no more of the Requiem. Because of this André felt himself strengthened in his view that they were concerned with an older composition.

The contradictions could not be greater: the family tradition, according to which Mozart worked on the Requiem up to his last days; André's thesis that the work is an arrangement or parody of an older compo-

[38] André, Preface; Abert II, 1026.

[39] In the original, "1790"; 1791 is unquestionably meant, since Zawrzel mentions in the same sentence *Die Zauberflöte, Tito,* the coronation of the Emperor, and Mozart's death.

[40] Communicated by Weber in *Cäcilia,* VI (1827), 193.

sition; Weber's opinion that no work of Mozart's was concerned at all but a piece patched together by Süssmayr from Mozartean memoranda; Mozart's own dating of 1792; the statements of neutral witnesses that the Requiem was already (in great part) in Count Walsegg's hands in August 1791 and was performed in September. André's and Weber's views can definitely be dismissed: the original score is not older than 1791 and its existence guarantees that (at least up to the end of the Offertory) it deals with Mozart's own work. Mozart's autograph dating is refuted by the date of his death. There remains therefore the question whether the family tradition can be brought together in any way with the statements of Zawrzel and Krüchten. This does not seem utterly impossible. It would be conceivable that from the time he received the commission in July until into August Mozart in his swift way composed the portions available in his autograph, finished outlines for the remaining movements, and turned over the whole thing to Eybler and Süssmayr for quick completion. Countess Walsegg, for whose memorial ceremony the Requiem was to be performed, had died in January 1791. The Count apparently did not want to wait any longer. Mozart was preoccupied by the extremely pressing and lucrative commission for *Tito* (the opera, with Süssmayr's help, is said to have been finished and rehearsed in eighteen days) and by the pressing need to complete *Die Zauberflöte*. Is it not conceivable that he looked over the completing of the Requiem by Eybler-Süssmayr only once in a while but that he turned his attention again to finishing the work after the performance of *Die Zauberflöte* (September 30, 1791) freed him from the most pressing labors? This would explain why the Requiem could have been available complete in large parts in August and performed in September and why Mozart still could have worked on it during his last days. This is no more than a hypothesis, but a hypothesis that would enable the contradictions to be resolved, the dating problem to approach a solution, and the Requiem to preserve its historical place as Mozart's "swan song." And is not a hypothesis, even a rather daring one, better than accusing the survivors of fraud or the unbiased witnesses of false testimony?

It is certain that research must abdicate before the task of clearing up, once and for all, all the problems connected with the Requiem. The circuit of the known sources, autograph, copies, printed editions, letters, and reports has been traveled many times. For other works the latest research has made many an astonishing discovery in hitherto unknown or incompletely investigated sources. For the Requiem, unfortunately, this cannot be awaited, because whatever there was of sketches in Mozart's legacy surely all went to Süssmayr, who would have destroyed them after using them. Even the shrewd André could turn up nothing, and the large portion of the legacy that he had bought in 1799 must have contained nothing for the Requiem; with his diligence and zeal he would surely not have let it escape him.

With respect to the instrumentation problem complete resignation is called for. A lucky discovery here and there may yet contribute to the dating problem. The problem of authenticity resolves itself in the end to a question of method of historical music-research, which may be summed up (in oversimplified brevity) in the formulation: source-philology or style-criticism? The new collected editions of the great masters have presented many an occasion to raise the question. The one method is not practicable without the other; they must complement one another. The Requiem, however, constitutes a test case for the methods. Since the first doubts arose about 1800, questions have been directed (quite rightly) at the sources, only to receive again and again the answer that for large parts of the work the sources alone are unable to furnish any definite information about the extent of Mozart's contribution. Against this negative result there is the unassailable, positive situation that the largest portion of the controversial movements, above all the *Lacrimosa,* Benedictus, and Agnus, from the standpoint of style and quality reveal the hand of Mozart with practically complete certainty. Let it be asked once more, concretely: if Mozart did not write them, who did? Süssmayr? From Stadler, Silverstolpe, and Novello down to the present it has been objected again and again that he was not capable of it. But if this question cannot be answered positively, then the conclusion must unequivocally be: "So long as it cannot be proved who composed or could have composed the doubtful portions the source-philological method is at a dead end, and speaking in place of it is the stylistic evidence that except for unimportant additions and except for the instrumentation the Requiem was composed by Mozart."[41] Since, however, methodological consistency is not to be found in everyone, there will no doubt be future occasions to say: Requiem but no peace.

[41] This is the conclusion I drew already in 1932, and I consider it still unshaken today. While the present article was being set in type, E. Hess's *Zur Ergänzung des Requiems durch Süssmayr* appeared in the *Mozart-Jahrbuch 1959,* pp. 99-108. I agree with the author's remarks on the instrumentation problem, but am not convinced by his criticism of the authenticity of the later movements.

POSTSCRIPT

More than a year after the first publication of the above study, a discovery of the greatest consequence was made known by Wolfgang Plath, of Augsburg, at the Congress of the Gesellschaft für Musikforschung in Kassel in October 1962. It was nothing less than the first presentation of a sheet of sketches for the Requiem. It contains a sketch for the *Rex tremendae majestatis* as well as the exposition of an Amen fugue (not used in the Requiem) that was perhaps intended to form the close of the Sequence. Because there is on the same sheet a fragment for *Die Zauberflöte*, it can be dated September-October 1791. While only this one sheet has turned up so far (according to Plath further discoveries are not entirely excluded), it demonstrates 1) that Einstein's view, that aside from the Vienna autograph nothing for the Requiem exists in Mozart's handwriting, was wrong; 2) that the oft-mentioned "slips of paper" actually existed; and 3) that Mozart's work on the Requiem really does belong to the year 1791. Thus the conclusions drawn in the above study receive strong confirmation, and the assumption that Süssmayr completed the composition (not the instrumentation) not independently but with the aid of Mozartean sketches and instructions is for the first time supported by documentary evidence. Moreover, if Süssmayr's statement that Mozart "discussed" the work with him "very often" fits the facts, it is difficult to see why he should not also have been in a position to use textless sketches as well (the one for the *Rex tremendae* presented by Plath has no text). Plath's contribution (*Über Skizzen zu Mozarts Requiem*) will be published in the Report of the Congress. I am grateful to Dr. Plath for letting me see his manuscript and for a photostat of the sheet of sketches.

*(Translated by Nathan Broder)*

# THE MELODIC SOURCES OF
# MOZART'S MOST POPULAR *LIED*

## By FREDERICK W. STERNFELD

T HE great creative productivity of Mozart's last years was strongly influenced by a revival of his enthusiasm for the music of Johann Sebastian Bach. There had been a previous stage of this enthusiasm when, in his middle twenties, he had seriously studied Bach at the home of Baron van Swieten. Then, in the spring of 1789, Mozart visited Leipzig and its Thomas-Kirche, and the impact of Bach's art, perhaps prepared for by that earlier occasion, proved to be both more profound and more extensive. To students of Mozart in the 20th century the *Requiem* and *Die Zauberflöte* are the obvious tokens of this neo-Baroque phase at the climax of the composer's career. The influence of the Thomas cantor on a work of liturgical music is both patent and natural. It is more surprising in the case of a decidedly popular fairy opera. Still, there is no escaping the fact that both the first and the last of the pieces composed by Mozart for *Die Zauberflöte* stand in the shadow of Bach's polyphony. The first piece, if we are to accept Aloys Fuchs's plausible hypothesis (Abert II, 810),[1] is the song of the two armored men, being a quotation of a chorale, and treated in the manner of a Bach cantata or motet. The second piece is the Overture, written just before the performance, and heralding, in its famous fugato, a degree of seriousness that must have come as a distinct surprise to Schikaneder's audience in Vienna's suburban theater, the "Theater auf der Wieden." There is hardly any up-to-date study of Mozart that does not trace these pieces to Bach. When Saint-Foix (V, 231) exclaims over the chorale of the two armored men: "Au milieu de tant de merveilles ... nous donne l'impression que Jean Sébastian Bach, lui-même, va paraître, je ne sais par quel sortilège," he epitomizes present-day stylistic analysis and highlights the contrast with the attitude of the 19th century when Jahn began his discussion by devoting five pages to the mysterious, solemn, and contrapuntal character of both the Overture and the chorale

---

[1] For complete bibliographical references see the list at the end of this article.

of the armored men without once mentioning Bach's name (Jahn II, 315-20). It may not be amiss, therefore, to resurrect an 18th-century source that constitutes one of the main reports of Mozart's visit to Leipzig and establishes yet another connection between a chorale used by Bach and a melody in *Die Zauberflöte*.

In 1798, in its first season of publication, the Leipzig periodical *Allgemeine musikalische Zeitung* offered its readers "Authenticated Anecdotes from Mozart's Life, a contribution towards the proper knowledge of this man as a human being and as artist," by Friedrich Rochlitz, editor of the journal and a former student of Cantor Doles at the Thomas-Schule. True, Rochlitz was a writer and a journalist who was not above prettifying an anecdote (Jahn I, iv); however, the substance of his account has been accepted by such reliable scholars as Jahn (II, 417), Abert (II, 628), Saint-Foix (V, 15), and Spitta (II, 611). During his sojourn in Leipzig Mozart visited the Thomas-Kirche and heard the choir, under the direction of Cantor Doles, perform Bach's motet for double chorus, *Singet dem Herrn ein neues Lied*.

The chorus had hardly sung a few measures when Mozart exclaimed "What is this?" and now all his soul seemed to be in his ears. And when the singing was over he exclaimed, full of joy, "That, after all, is something from which one may learn." He was told that this school, at which Sebastian Bach had been cantor, possessed a complete collection of his motets and preserved them as a kind of sacred relic. "That is right, that is good," he exclaimed, "show them to me." But one had no scores of these vocal compositions, consequently he asked for the parts. And now it was a joy for the quiet observer to see Mozart sit, all intensity, distributing the parts around him [holding some] in his hands, [putting others] on his knees and on the chairs around him, and not rise until he had scanned everything of Bach that was there.

In the motet that Doles chose for Mozart's hearing the chorale *Nun lob mein Seel den Herren* looms large. Just why Doles selected this particular work is not stated or, for that matter, why there should have been this special performance for Mozart's benefit. Jahn, Abert, and Saint-Foix make the reasonable assumption that Doles was paying a musical debt, since earlier Mozart had obliged his Leipzig hosts by a brilliant performance on the organ at the Thomas-Kirche. On this occasion "Doles was wholly delighted with Mozart's playing and believed old Sebastian Bach, his teacher, had risen from the grave.

Mozart . . . improvised magnificently on every theme given . . . among others on the chorale *Jesus, meine Zuversicht.*"[2]

Now, the motet *Singet dem Herrn ein neues Lied* is 368 measures long and consists of four parts. The first part (mm. 1-151) is a paraphrase of Psalm 149. The second (mm. 151-220) is a treatment of the third stanza of the chorale *Nun lob mein Seel den Herren.* The third (mm. 221-255) and fourth (255-368) parts are a paraphrase of Psalm 150. The second part is of crucial interest to us, because it is the only extensive treatment of a chorale by Bach of which we can say with certainty that it was known to Mozart. Whether or not Mozart knew Bach's cantatas and chorale preludes is problematical. In fact, the only other documented source for Mozart's knowledge of Protestant chorales and their employment as *cantus firmi* is the treatise *Die Kunst des reinen Satzes.* This work by Bach's devoted pupil Kirnberger gives the actual melodic source of the chorale of the armored men (Abert II, 819). Unlike the contrapuntal technique of this striking passage, as well as of so many of Bach's motets and cantatas, the motet *Singet dem Herrn* does not absorb the chorale melody in slow note values in the polyphonic texture. Rather, it is sung in a straightforward manner, harmonized in four parts, the melody in the soprano in quarter notes and duple measure. The motet as a whole is scored for eight voices, subdivided into a first and second chorus of four parts each. The chorale is allotted to the second chorus, and each of its lines is antiphonally answered by the first chorus, which sings polyphonically. The result is that the melody of the chorale impresses itself upon the listener with unusual clarity.

It is a melody that is first recorded in a collection of German Protestant songs by Johann Kugelmann printed at Augsburg in 1540. The collection contains thirty-nine polyphonic arrangements of various melodies, four of them of the melody *Nun lob mein Seel den Herren* (Zahn V, 72 f.; VI, 19, Source No. 60). It has been plausibly suggested (Winterfeld I, 209) that Kugelmann was the author not only of the arrangements but also of the melody itself. With its major tonality, its triple rhythm, and its dance-like character this tune sounds very much like a variation of some German folksong. German folklore altogether was a treasure ground to which the Lutheran musicians of the 16th

---

[2] This anecdote is recounted by Rochlitz in the *Allgemeine musikalische Zeitung* of 1801 (Leitzmann 149) and by Reichardt, with additional details, in the first volume of his Berlin periodical *Musikalische Zeitung* (Jahn III, 228 f.). Reichardt spells the chorale "Jesu meine Zuversicht" and not "Jesus . . ." The latter spelling is necessary to locate the tune in modern works of reference, such as those of Winterfeld and Terry.

century frequently had recourse in order to build up their new, vernacular liturgy. Historians of German Protestant church music, in characterizing this tune, employ such phrases as "folk-tone" and "dance-like" and speak, in summing up, of "one of the most rapid-moving [*bewegtesten*], joyous, festive melodies of Protestant church-song, the work of a competent, intelligent composer, creating in the popular vein" (Winterfeld I, 209; III, 34). The tune was widely known in the 17th century, and beginning with the 18th century it entered into general circulation. Bach used the chorale ten times, and in the following tabulation I have taken particular care to indicate which versions were readily available in Mozart's lifetime. In this connection it is well to remember that the only publications between 1752 *(Kunst der Fuge)* and 1801 *(Wohltemperiertes Clavier)* to bear Johann Sebastian Bach's name on the title-page were two editions of his Chorales, both with a preface by C. P. E. Bach. The first was published by Birnstiel in 1765-69, the second by Breitkopf in 1784-87 (Bach Reader, 270). Here, then, is the tabulation, of which items (6) and (7) are particularly noteworthy:

(1) Cantata No. 17. Published 1765, Birnstiel I, No. 7; 1784, Breitkopf I, No. 6; Bach II, 225 f.; Terry, No. 276. Text: "Wie sich ein Vat'r erbarmet," i.e., the third stanza of *Nun lob mein Seel den Herren.*

(2) Cantata No. 28. Published: Bach, Vol. V, Part I, 258-65. Text: "Nun lob mein Seel den Herren." Here the chorale is extensively treated in motet-like fashion; at its end Bach notes in the MS, "174 Takte" as if to emphasize its length; Bach later re-arranged this chorus for a motet (cf. No. 7 in this tabulation), and in this form Mozart may have studied it in Leipzig.

(3) Cantata No. 29. Published: 1769, Birnstiel II, No. 121; 1785, Breitkopf II, No. 116; Bach, Vol. V, Part I, 316-20; Terry No. 279. Text: "Sei Lob und Preis mit Ehren," i.e., the fifth stanza of *Nun lob mein Seel den Herren.*

(4) Cantata No. 51. Published: Bach, Vol. XII, Part II, 14-19. Text: "Sei Lob und Preis mit Ehren," as in (3).

(5) Cantata No. 167. Published: Bach XXXIII, 140-46. Text: "Sei Lob und Preis mit Ehren," as in (3) and (4).

(6) Motet *Singet dem Herrn* (Schmieder No. 225). Published: Bach XXXIX, 18-26. Text: "Wie sich ein Vat'r erbarmet," as in (1). This is the motet that Doles conducted for Mozart in 1789, as discussed in the body of this article.

(7) Motet *Sei Lob und Preis mit Ehren* (Schmieder No. 231). Published: Bach XXXIX, 167-172. Text: fifth stanza, as in (3), (4), and (5). A re-working by Bach of (3), inserted into a motet by Telemann (Schmieder, Anhang, No. 160). In this form Mozart may have heard this arrangement of the chorale in Leipzig. When F. Wüllner edited the motets for the Bach-Gesellschaft (date of his preface is 1892), one of his main sources was the part-books of the Thomas-Schule in Leipzig. There survive three such sets of part-books and two of these three con-

tain the Telemann motet (*Jauchzet dem Herrn alle Welt*). In the second set, which dates from the 1780's, the composition bears, at its beginning, the rubric "di Telemann, v. Joh. Seb. Bach verbessert," and at the beginning of the chorale "von Joh. Seb. Bach allein," (p. xvi f. and p. xxiv of Wüllner's preface). This set of parts also contains two motets entirely by Bach, namely, *Singet dem Herrn* — the *pièce de résistance* of our discussion — and *Komm, Jesu, komm;* and, in addition, a generous number of motets by Doles. One suspects, therefore, that this second set must have been among those used by Doles in 1789, particularly so since its first 21 numbers are written in the same hand and contain (6) and (7) as well as Doles's own compositions.

(8) Chorale *Nun lob, mein Seel, den Herren* (Schmieder, No. 389). Published: 1786, Breitkopf III, No. 268; Terry, No. 277.

(9) Chorale *Nun lob, mein Seel, den Herren* (Schmieder, No. 390). Published: 1787, Breitkopf IV, No. 295; Terry, No. 278.

(10) Organ Prelude *Nun lob, mein Seel, den Herren* (Schmieder, Anhang, No. 60). It is doubtful whether this composition is by Bach; sometimes it is attributed to Krebs.

In summing up this tabulation, it is certain that Mozart heard (6) and likely that he heard (7); and it is possible that he knew one or more of four simple arrangements of the same melody that were published during his lifetime, namely (1), (3), (8), and (9).

Another factor needs to be considered, namely, that the melody of *Nun lob* usually occurs in triple rhythm during the 17th and 18th centuries. Of the four simple versions just mentioned only one is in duple time. But, in the version that Mozart undoubtedly knew—(6) (as well as (7) which he may have known also) — the melody is treated in duple time, in even note values, as is Papageno's *Lied*. Below, then, is the soprano part as it appears in (6):

Ex. 1

We now append lines 7-8 of the chorale, transposed from B-flat major to F major, and the opening of Papageno's *Lied, Ein Mädchen oder Weibchen*:

Ex. 2

The similarity of these two four-measure phrases is, naturally, much too obvious to have escaped attention, and in 1840 Robert Schumann, then editor of the bi-weekly *Neue Zeitschrift für Musik* of Leipzig, published a short note by Karl Ferdinand Becker on the last page of a four-page issue. Becker had traced the melody to the chorale, though he did not connect the chorale with Bach. In order to understand both his discovery and his emphases, we must remember that Becker was organist at Leipzig's Nicolai-Kirche and a music historian, and that in both of these capacities he exhibited a particular interest in chorales. Among his publications are such titles as *The Collections of Chorales of the Various Christian Churches*, 1845; *J. S. Bach's Four-Part Chorales*, 1843; and *Protestant Chorale Book*, 1844. Becker was somewhat of a 19th-century antiquarian whose considerable merit lies in the data he amassed rather than in his evaluation of them. Einstein observed in Riemann's *Musiklexikon* that Becker was "a diligent collector, but no scholar." To paraphrase and summarize Becker's note:

The tunes of Mozart's *Zauberflöte* in several instances are derived from other composers. Did not Mozart consciously derive the song of the armored men from a chorale, three centuries old? It took decades to discover this — Gerber "to my knowledge" was the first to publicize it in 1812. Small wonder, then, that another half century passed before the further discovery was made that the Papageno tune agrees, note for note, with the 7th and 8th lines of the chorale *Nun lob mein Seel den Herren*, by Scandello, who died at Dresden in 1580. This latter derivation was undoubtedly unconscious on the composer's part, but there was one in the audience who took the two lines of Scandello and the additional two lines of Mozart and fitted the whole to Hölty's sentimental text, "Ueb immer Treu und Redlichkeit."

Becker's note, entitled *Mozart and Scandello*, actually takes up three distinct points: one regarding the armored men; the second about Scandello's chorale; and the third about the contrafactum of Mozart's melody with Hölty's text. As to the chorale of the armored men, its origin was mentioned in 1798 by Rochlitz, in the same set of anecdotes that reports Mozart's enthusiasm for the motet *Singet dem Herrn ein neues Lied* (Leitzmann 144; Jahn III, 318). Still, Becker's remark has merit because it stresses the absorption of *another* chorale into *Die Zauberflöte* and distinguishes between the conscious and unconscious process of melodic borrowing.

Modern scholars derive the melody from Kugelmann. Just where Scandello comes in I have been unable to determine. Winterfeld, Wüllner, Zahn, and Terry all name Kugelmann's collection as the first printed source; none of them even mentions Scandello in this connection. One suspects that Mozart knew neither of these two Protestant composers of the 16th century. On the other hand, it is surprising that Becker overlooked the connection with Bach, particularly the one piece of Bach's church music that Mozart definitely knew. Later historians rarely reprint Becker's hypothesis, probably owing to the lack of any connection between Scandello and Mozart. Without committing himself further, Jahn (III, 284) says of Papageno's song that "it has been remarked that the beginning is identical with the seventh and eighth lines of Scandello's chorale." Hyatt King (p. 252) states: "Jahn remarked that the melody of a chorale by Scandello was the counterpart, in long note values, of Papageno's *Ein Mädchen oder Weibchen*. Chantavoine has noted an even more interesting parallel in Haydn's *Mondo della Luna*. It hardly seems possible to ascribe both these to mere coincidence." Abert, Dent, and Saint-Foix do not mention Becker's speculation.

With regard to Becker's remarks on Hölty's text, it must be remembered that Becker wrote for a German public, and that every schoolchild in Germany and Austria would naturally associate Mozart's tune with the Hölty text, for that is the way the melody has been printed in school song-books and other popular collections for over a century. In fact, the text in itself shows many composite influences, both German and English.

The tendency to disregard Becker's hypothesis seems to have begun in 1902, when the dean of historians of German song, Max Friedländer, published his monumental *Das deutsche Lied im 18. Jahrhundert*. Friedländer properly stresses that in order to evaluate Mozart as a composer of *Lieder*, we must also consider the lyrical songs inserted in his operas, from the time of *Die Entführung* to *Die Zauberflöte.* Some of these have achieved an even greater popularity than his individual songs. Of all of Mozart's melodies, that for *Ein Mädchen oder Weibchen* has become "by far the best known. The reason for this is that Hölty's text was fitted to it; Hölty's verse with Mozart's melody has been distributed among the masses . . . The carillon of the Potsdam Garnisonkirche plays it still today [1902] on the half hour" (II, 268, 471). There can be no doubt that Friedländer's assessment of the popularity of this *Lied* for German-speaking countries is accurate. Even Saint-Foix (V, 236) states cautiously of *Ein Mädchen:* "peut-être, celui qui est demeuré le plus populaire de tous les thèmes de la *Flûte enchantée.*" Friedländer (I, 300) derives the tune from a German folksong, *Es freit ein wilder Wassermann,* and certainly a secular song with a text that speaks of wooing seems, on the surface at least, a much more likely guess than a church chorale by Scandello.

Hermann Abert discusses the melody's derivation in his great Mozart work, published in 1919-21. In the body of the text (II, 708) he merely states that the melody is founded "on old German folk-treasure," but a footnote refers to Friedländer's folksong as well as to operatic works of Paisiello, Galuppi, and Grétry. Abert does not contradict Friedländer, he merely amplifies his suggestions, for he stresses the facts that the three excerpts quoted by him are all "volksmässig," "volks-tümlich," and "im Volkston." Abert thus suggested the shift from mere folksong to "folksong-like" operatic song, and Chantavoine's *Mozart dans Mozart* (1948) adduces in Haydn an even more likely model than Galuppi, Paisiello, or Grétry. This is sound reasoning in view of Haydn's thoroughly German melodic contours; what could be more German than *Die Zauberflöte,* the arias of the Queen of the Night notwithstanding? Hyatt King is quite right in preferring Chantavoine's candidate, if the candidate must be an operatic composer.

But the difficulty with the analogies adduced by Friedländer and his successors is that their melodic similarities extend only to two measures, whereas the relevant passage from the Bach chorale is four measures long. I give below the musical quotations from Friedländer, Abert, and Hyatt King.[3] In the case of Friedländer, I have extended his two-measure quotation by reference to his own *Hundert Volkslieder* (p. 61)

[3] There are many songs that leap from the dominant to the tonic and depart from the tonic only to return to it. One other Bach chorale shows the same two-measure phrase (*In allen meinen Taten,* Terry No. 192), and the melodic indices for Bach by May de Forest Payne and the general indices by Barlow and Morgenstern list many similar melodies. In no instance does the similarity extend to four measures.

and in Hyatt King's case I have extended his two-measure excerpt by reference to Mark Lothar's vocal score for Haydn's *Welt auf dem Monde* (p. 23).

Ex. 3

To summarize now our own opinion concerning the derivation of Mozart's melody: The experience of hearing and studying Bach's motets in the spring of 1789 was of decisive importance for Mozart. Obviously, that experience was very much alive in 1791 when he wrote the contrapuntal passages in the Requiem, the fugato in the Overture to *Die Zauberflöte,* and the contrapuntal passage in the finale of the opera where the chorale of the armored men serves as the *cantus firmus* (Fischer 47). Is it not reasonable, then, to assume that the melodies employed in Bach's motet, *Singet dem Herrn ein neues Lied* continued to linger in Mozart's memory, particularly the tune of the chorale to which Bach gives such prominence? We have a by-product, one may say, of Mozart's enthusiasm for Bach's motet in that the four-measure phrase from the chorale in the motet serves as a melodic source for Papageno's popular song.

This finding in no way precludes acknowledgment of the two-measure phrases referred to by Friedländer, Abert, and Hyatt King, as subsidiary sources. Both the two-measure phrase and the four-measure phrase are, after all, common enough in their melodic contours. One must agree with Winterfeld that the melody of the chorale is "folksong-like," if not actually derived from a folksong. It is possible that a German folksong of the Renaissance is the common ancestor of Kugelmann's chorale, Friedländer's secular song, and the melody in Haydn's *opera buffa.* In fact, the melodic similarity to a variety of songs current in the 18th century undoubtedly enhanced the popularity of Papageno's tune.

BIBLIOGRAPHY

Abert             Hermann Abert, *W. A. Mozart*, 2 vols., Leipzig, 1919-21.

Bach              *J. S. Bachs Werke*, 46 Jahrgänge in 59 vols., Leipzig, 1851-99.

Bach Reader       H. T. David & A. Mendel, *The Bach Reader*, New York, 1945.

Becker            Karl F. Becker, *Mozart und Scandelli*, in *Neue Zeitschrift für Musik*, XII (1840), 112.

Birnstiel         *J. S. Bachs vierstimmige Choralgesänge gesammelt von C. P. E. Bach*, 2 vols., Leipzig, 1765-69.

Breitkopf         *J. S. Bachs vierstimmige Choralgesänge*, 4 vols., Leipzig, 1784-87.

Dent              Edward J. Dent, *Mozart's Operas*, 2nd ed., London, 1947.

Fischer           Wilhelm Fischer, *Der, welcher wandelt diese Strasse voll Beschwerden*, in *Mozart-Jahrbuch 1950*, Salzburg, 1951, pp. 41-48.

Friedländer I     Max Friedländer, *Das deutsche Lied im 18. Jahrhundert*, 2 vols. in 3, Stuttgart, 1902.

Friedländer II    *Hundert deutsche Volkslieder*, ed. M. Friedländer, Leipzig, [pref.] 1886.

Hyatt King        A. Hyatt King, *The Melodic Sources and Affinities of Die Zauberflöte*, in *The Musical Quarterly*, XXXVI (1950); 241-58.

Jahn              Otto Jahn, *Life of Mozart*, tr. P. D. Townsend, 3 vols., London, 1891.

Leitzmann         *W. A. Mozarts Leben in . . . Berichten der Zeitgenossen*, ed. Albert Leitzmann, Leipzig, 1926.

Saint-Foix        T. de Wyzewa & G. de Saint-Foix, *W. A. Mozart*, 5 vols., Paris, 1912-46.

Schmieder         *Them.-Syst. Verzeichnis der . . . Werke von J. S. Bach*, ed. Wolfgang Schmieder, Leipzig, 1950.

Spitta            Philipp Spitta, *Life of Bach*, tr. C. Bell & J. A. Fuller-Maitland, 2nd ed., 3 vols., London, 1899.

Terry             *The Four-Part Chorals of J. S. Bach*, ed. Charles Sanford Terry, 5 parts, London, 1929.

Winterfeld        Karl von Winterfeld, *Der evangelische Kirchengesang*, 3 vols., Leipzig, 1843-47.

Zahn              Johannes Zahn, *Die Melodien der deutschen evangelischen Kirchenlieder*, 6 vols., Gütersloh, 1889-93.

# THE FIRST GUIDE TO MOZART

## By NATHAN BRODER

IN the Library of Congress there is a thin volume called *Anweisung zum genauen Vortrage der Mozartschen Clavierconcerte/hauptsächlich in Absicht richtiger Applicatur* ("Guide to the accurate performance of the Mozartean Piano Concertos/ principally with respect to correct fingering"). It was written by A. E. Müller and published at Leipzig by Breitkopf & Härtel in 1796. This small work has received scant attention in the Mozart literature. Girdlestone does not mention it in his excellent monograph on the concertos[1]; Dennerlein[2] merely lists it; Saint-Foix[3] says of it only that it is a "very curious and serious work on the interpretation of the master's concertos"; and, most recently, Hyatt King[4] describes it briefly. Since the Guide is, so far as I know, the first publication to be devoted to any aspect of Mozart's work, and since it appeared only five years after his death, an examination of it and some information about its author may be of interest.

August Eberhard Müller was born at Northeim in Hanover December 13, 1767. Not much is known of his early life. He studied for a time with Johann Christoph Friedrich Bach, ninth son of Johann Sebastian, at Bückeburg. In 1788 he settled down in Magdeburg. There he was active as pianist, flutist, organist, and conductor. A resident of Magdeburg, writing in the Berlin *Musikalische Zeitung* under date of November 18, 1793, remarks that the orchestra in his town up to now had been able to play only Pleyel's symphonies but that now it was capable of tackling Mozart. According to him, music

---

[1] C. M. Girdlestone, *Mozart's Piano Concertos*, London, 1948; Norman, Okla., 1952.

[2] Hanns Dennerlein, *Der unbekannte Mozart: Die Welt seiner Klavierwerke*, Leipzig, 1951, p. 196.

[3] G. de Saint-Foix, *W.-A. Mozart*, Vol. IV, Paris, 1939, p. 207.

[4] In his interesting and informative collection of studies, *Mozart in Retrospect*, London, 1955, p. 15.

in Magdeburg was fifty years behind the times and the public taste still ran more to "watery Dittersdorfian soups, prepared on the stage by keepers of cook-shops, than to strong Mozartean broths." He concludes, however, with the statement that the public is being gradually educated, thanks to Müller.[5] In 1794 Müller went to Leipzig as organist of the Nicolai-Kirche. During the next eight years he and his wife appeared frequently as pianists; both were admired especially for their performances of Mozart. Müller also served during this period as first flutist of the Gewandhaus Orchestra. Ten years after he arrived in Leipzig, Müller was appointed cantor of the Thomas-Schule, succeeding Johann Adam Hiller. In 1810 he was called to Weimar, as Kapellmeister of the court opera there. He was cordially received by Goethe, and the relations between the two men remained friendly and respectful until Müller's death on December 3, 1817. Several movements of Mozart's Requiem were performed at the funeral services.

During Müller's years in Leipzig he became an intimate friend of Gottfried Christoph Härtel. Breitkopf & Härtel not only published some of Müller's compositions but used him as an editor and arranger. They brought out his vocal scores of *Idomeneo, Die Entführung, Der Schauspieldirektor, Don Giovanni, Così fan tutte,* and the Requiem (G. A. Böhme in Hamburg published Müller's vocal score of *La Clemenza di Tito*). When Breitkopf & Härtel began their edition of Mozart's "Oeuvres complettes" in 1798, they called upon Müller for help, and he was so enthusiastic about working on the project that he asked not to be paid for it.[6] (He also had a hand in the same firm's "Oeuvres complettes" of Haydn.) It was most probably Müller who wrote, for this edition (*Cahier* 17, 1806), the last ten measures of Mozart's Fantasy in D minor, K. 397; in the first edition (1804, Vienna, Bureau d'Arts & d'Industrie) the work ends with the dominant chord in measure 97.[7] The Sonata in B-flat listed by Einstein as K. 498a (it is *Anh.* 136 in the second edition of Köchel) and still published in some current editions of Mozart sonatas was at least partly, and perhaps entirely, the work of Müller.[8]

[5] Günther Haupt, *A. E. Müller's Leben und Klavierwerke,* Leipzig, 1926, p. 9. Most of the biographical data given here are taken from this dissertation. See also Wilibald Nagel in *Die Musik, Jahrg.* IX (1909-10), *Heft* 20, p. 84.

[6] Haupt, *op. cit.,* p. 15.

[7] See Paul Hirsch, *A Mozart Problem,* in *Music and Letters,* XXV (1944), 209.

[8] See the American reprint of Köchel-Einstein, p. 1023, and Richard S. Hill, *The Plate Numbers of C. F. Peters' Predecessors,* in *Papers ... of the American Musicological Society ... Washington ... 1938,* p. 129.

Müller's *Anweisung* begins with a three-page introduction, a translation of which follows:

"At a time when *instrumental music* has been raised by various distinguished men of genius to a height it has never before achieved, when, too, admiration for this category of art and virtuosity therein have received such an extraordinary impetus, a study intended not to present new inventions and discoveries nor to offer new acquisitions in the blossoming field of instrumental music but to secure that which is already written, to make it generally more useful, to render its treasures more generally available — such a study may surely hope for a not entirely unfavorable reception. Among the instruments, however, for which the great masters of recent and modern times have written so excellently, the clavier stands out from more than one point of view. Since the time when the piano, especially, supplanted the cold, stolid, insensitive harpsichord, when the celebrated Stein, formerly in Augsburg, was able, by transforming its structure and by other improvements, to give this instrument a sufficiently strong tone while retaining all its softness and flexibility, it — and with it the compositions, especially the concertos, written for it — has become so generally accepted in the public musical entertainments as perhaps never before.

"This firm and estimable predilection, supported by a friendly and beneficial Nature, brought forth and aroused in most recent times various very fortunate cultivators of this class of music, and, since we are dealing here only with *clavier concertos,* among those cultivators *one* especially, quite extraordinary and prominent above all his rivals — need I say that this was Mozart? This excellent man, whom Germany only began to honor sufficiently when he was dead, united in his clavier concertos great abundance and novelty of harmony with lovely, often caressing, melody; great richness, often boldness, of fantasy in general, uncommon variety, pomp and brilliance of a full, completely worked-out accompaniment with the mellowing gentleness and grace of the wind instruments. In his solos he gave the virtuosos enough opportunity to display their powers brilliantly; but he never demanded impossibilities of them, and for that reason deliberately wrote throughout as performably, as *practically* as — perhaps the only one to do so besides him — the great *Philipp Emanuel Bach.*

"As surely as I hope that great crowds of connoisseurs, amateurs, and virtuosos will applaud my view of Mozart's works in the category we are discussing — in so far as that view concerns the qualities listed first above; as surely as I can imagine that many will extend the catalogue of the highly praised merits of the Mozartean clavier concertos by who knows how many items, and in the process of deifying him will forget that he was human — so surely do I also know, taught by experience, that my last assertion will be denied. From all sides one hears complaints about the unplayable passages in the Mozartean concertos, about how they are contrary to all natural finger-placement; consequently, about how they are either quite unusable or at least very uncertain in performance. In answer to these complaints, I take the liberty of asserting that all the roughness, imprecision, uncertainty, looseness, and lack of control in the performance of these concertos is the fault only of an unnatural, false, or quite neglected and wavering fingering by the player, which is created often for the convenience of the beginner in clavier-playing but far more often by the only too common ignorance or carelessness of the teacher.

"No special evidence need be adduced for this apparently harsh statement; in my opinion it is sufficiently proved by the facts presented from beginning to end of this very volume. If I am not mistaken, the chief failure of the usual fingering — indeed I may say of every non-Bachian, or, what is the same thing, non-Mozartean fingering — is the too infrequent or incorrect use of the fourth and fifth fingers. That great Hamburg theorist and practical musician already saw this, and in his *Versuch über die wahre Art das Clavier zu spielen* worked energetically against both the neglect of the thumb or first finger and the arrogance of the second and third fingers and their strong tendency to suppress the two last ones. He also wrote for the benefit of the latter fingers his fine Sonata in F minor in that *Versuch;* but for some virtuosos and amateurs this work is too expensive, while the rest consider it old music, indeed stale merchandise; they have no taste for the essential quality of this music and consequently do not derive from it the values that they could derive from it. It is true that Herr Musikdirektor Türk in Halle has published a less costly work on this subject, his *Klavierschule für Lehrer und Lernende;* but it contains nothing special with respect to today's new figures and passages and, as regards the more general rules, nothing that Bach did not say long ago.

"It seems to me, therefore, that there is still a gap among the practical guides to well-grounded clavier-playing. It seems to me that we have lacked up to now a book that would present within a modest frame — in order to avoid expense — the irrefutable rules of the Bachian fingering, that would apply them to the latest figures and passages, and by means of enough examples elucidate those compositions of this sort that are rightly treasured most and are just now most sought after. To fill this gap as well as I can is the purpose of the present volume. Anyone who has mastered Bach will find him again everywhere in my Guide; anyone who has not known him or has neglected him up to now will no doubt find the study of these movements with the fingering set down above them difficult; for what of importance is learned without effort? But to comfort and encourage such a one I can predict that when he has finally mastered it all accurately and firmly, he too will be able to play all Mozartean concertos — indeed all correctly and well-written concertos — rightly and with security, since the amateur will find here *all* the important and difficult passages of *all* the Mozartean concertos that are published and since one can scarcely imagine an important figure that is not in Mozart or at least that would remain troublesome to one who plays all of Mozart. I have chosen all the works of this master exclusively as a basis, for the reason given above.

"For the convenience of the player I have also indicated for each concerto the theme and the number of the pages and lines.

"This Guide appears in two books, which are published one immediately after the other: Leipzig in September 1796.

August Eberhard Müller
Organist in the Nicolai-Kirche"

This introduction is followed by twenty-four pages of music, comprising passages from five of Mozart's piano concertos, in the following order: A major, K. 414; F major, K. 413; C major, K. 415; B-flat major, K. 595; and D major, K. 451. These passages are carefully fingered, and occasionally Müller adds a comment. For example on page 12 he writes: "Most clavier-players place the second finger on the upper [i. e. black] keys in chromatic runs, but this fingering is not recommended because the second finger must be placed now on the under key, now on the upper, as is the case in every progression from E to F and from B to C. But if the third finger is placed at once on the upper keys, this is avoided, and the second finger is required only for F and C while the third finger is reserved for the upper keys." In connection with the following passage from the first movement of K. 413 (m. 219):

Ex. 1

Müller remarks: "Passages of this sort are usually played thus:

Ex. 2

But that fingering in which the third finger is used on the B before C is to be preferred to this one, because it does away with the frequent over and under motion of the second finger and the hand plays more quietly. Mozart himself used this fingering in such cases."

At the bottom of page 24 appears this note: "Ende des ersten Hefts." According to Hyatt King,[9] the second volume mentioned in the introduction was never published.

\*     \*

\*

Just how Müller knew that Mozart used a particular fingering is not clear. Müller seems never to have set foot outside of North and Central Germany, and there is no evidence of any personal contact between him and Mozart. It is possible, of course, that he went from Magdeburg to Leipzig or Berlin to hear Mozart when the latter traveled to the Prussian capital in the spring of 1789, but there is no proof of it. In any case, it is plain enough from all of the foregoing that he revered the master deeply. The abundant Mozartisms in his own earlier piano pieces and songs are a further indication of this, if any were needed. It is not certain that Müller was responsible for the many changes in phrasing and other details of the Mozart "Oeuvres complettes" — changes that were later incorporated in the *Gesamtausgabe* and the Breitkopf & Härtel "Urtext" edition of the piano works — but if he was, it must be remembered that he was twelve years younger than Mozart and came to maturity during a time of rapid transition to the new "taste" of the Beethoven era. According to Haupt, the Mozart influence disappears in Müller's late works. What is of value

[9] *Loc. cit.*

to us in the *Anweisung* of 1796 is the additional light it throws on the status of Mozart five years after his death and the corroboration it offers of certain facts that have not been universally accepted or that are not yet well known — the complete triumph of the piano over the harpsichord before the end of the 18th century, at least in Germany; the recognized pre-eminence of Mozart in the field of the piano concerto; the technical difficulties, due to the use of old-fashioned fingerings for these modern works, that prevented them from being still more widely known; and the great lag in the acceptance of modern fingering, still not generally used more than forty years after its principles had been laid down by Philipp Emanuel Bach.

# SOME FALLACIES IN
# MOZART BIOGRAPHY

By OTTO ERICH DEUTSCH

THIS warning comes too late for the flood of new writings on Mozart, which could hardly wait for the year 1956 to begin. Even in normal times new biographies of great composers might incur censure for being mere repetitions of thrice-told tales. Among the experts on music it is precisely the musicians who, being ill qualified for historical and archival studies, inevitably turn to their predecessors when they find it necessary or desirable to write a new book on one of the masters. Unfortunately, they are equally ill qualified to judge which of their sources are reliable. These predecessors are even more dangerous for journalistic and fictionalized biographies, both of which have recently become so numerous. The authors of the former stand ready to produce a well-timed work on each and every master; thereby they often bring about distressing results. The dissemination of false notions among the public by books of the second type has perhaps a less devastating effect, but for the serious investigator who does not recognize the mixture of fact and fiction such works can be fatal. Finally, for those music lovers who are understandably reluctant to read biographies, there remains the innocent category of the pure novel, in the case of Mozart beginning with Heribert Rau (1858). Naturally the novelists depend upon biographies for their material; therefore, even if they are true artists, they contribute to the spreading of current errors. It is especially painful to find among the novelists some who are not artists but scholars, historians of music as well as of literature. And if these men on occasion find their way back to their own vocations, they produce hybrids that confuse not only laymen and screen-writers but also professional colleagues.

All this has been accelerated in the case of Mozart, although the foundations of Mozart biography, established by Otto Jahn as long ago as 1856, were perfectly sound. Hermann Abert, whose great contributions to our knowledge of Mozart were of another sort, already began to vitiate Jahn's work; this despite the fact that his biography of Mozart made good use of the research on details done prior to 1921. Some researchers were proud when they could correct Jahn in certain details, albeit one might think it a matter of course that in a hundred years some new knowledge would be added. On the other hand, the following little catalogue of errors both frequent and exceptional may indicate how much historical knowledge has either fallen into eclipse or failed to become prevalent.

Let us begin with the physical appearance of Mozart as it has come down to us in ten genuine and a hundred false or imaginary portraits. The childish desire of many biographers and collectors to discover and publish unknown portraits of great individuals has led in the case of Mozart to such a situation as the duping of many Mozart researchers in the first half of this century by a notorious forger of silhouettes named Josef Kuderna. In 1929 the *Mozart Jahrbuch* edited by Abert published a silhouette that Fritz Wagner had found in a collection in Thuringia. It shows a man standing and reading a book, a pose familiar to us from depictions of the Goethe circle. It is inscribed: "Leopold Mozart in the Dalberg house in Erfurt, reading the libretto of the opera Idomeneo rè di Creta composed by his son." Abert was puzzled, to be sure, by the hitherto unknown stay of the two Mozarts in Erfurt about 1781, the year when the opera was first performed. He adds, however, "On the other hand, any mystery concerning the picture itself seems improbable . . . At all events the silhouette is certainly old." It was at most twenty years old. At about the same time the Hungarian city of Raab (Györ) acquired from the collection of the one-armed pianist Géza Count Zichy a series of silhouettes that were supposed to have been formerly in the famous Lanna collection in Prague. Among the nine leaves were seven allegedly connected with Mozart, whose signature is awkwardly imitated on them and who is himself pictured in high, "cut-throat" collars. One leaf bears the legend: "True likeness of my father Leopold Mozart at a concert in the circle of music lovers in Raab, Hungary, made by the Countess Erdödy." The consequence of the acquisition by the Raab Museum was a seriously conceived article that Dr. Rudolf Galos published with illustrations in the scholarly magazine *Györ Szemle* (November-December, 1930). He determined the date of the Mozarts' hitherto unknown stay in Raab as 1768. Had he been acquainted with the aforementioned *Mozart Jahrbuch* he would have noted that father Mozart looked the same in Erfurt around 1781 as he did in Raab in 1768. Still another silhouette of Leopold and Wolfgang Mozart occasioned an article by Frau Adele Egger in the *Blätter für Heimatskunde* (1938) on "Mozart's Stay in Graz," a place where the two Mozarts had never been. Finally, Georg Schünemann published in the *Jahrbuch der Musikbibliothek Peters* (1940) a silhouette of Mozart, allegedly by his sister, which the Prussian State Library had acquired. These forgeries too stemmed from Kuderna's productive workshop.

But our intention was to speak of biographical errors that directly concern Mozart's life and work. For one thing there are the two Mesmers — the famous hypnotist Dr. Franz Anton and his cousin Josef, a school principal — who were friends of the Mozart family in Vienna. They have been repeatedly confused with one another, or even thought to be the same person, and their degree of kinship has been misunderstood. Among the Salzburg patrons of Mozart, the Burgomaster Sigmund Haffner is said to have ordered the Serenade K. 250 for the wedding of his daughter, although he was no longer living at the time. On the other hand, his son of the same name did order the Symphony K. 385 on the occasion of his elevation to the nobility. Another common error confuses the two Counts Esterházy in Vienna: Count Johann, who was one of the active friends of music among the high nobility and also Master of the Masonic lodge "Zur gekrönten Hoffnung," and Count Franz, known in his youth as Quinquin. The former was one of two noble members of that lodge who died within a short time of one another — it was for these two that Mozart wrote his *Masonic Funeral Music*. Futhermore, Count Franz Esterházy has also been repeatedly confused with his father and namesake, who had been director and supervisor of all theatrical productions in Vienna.

Among Mozart's piano pupils was Countess Marie Karoline Thiennes de Rumbecke (1755-1812), the sister of Chancellor Johann Philipp Count Cobenzl. It was he who built a country house on the Reisenberg, a hill in the Vienna woods later called the Cobenzl. Mozart occasionally visited there in 1781, once staying the night. Since, however, no Reisenberg could be found on the more recent maps, Abert (II, 21) transformed Mozart's own reference to the hill into Reichenberg, evidently the city in Bohemia. The distance was not so great between the Rothmühle near Schwechat, the summer place of the wealthy Frau Mesmer that Leopold and Wolfgang Mozart visited in 1781, and a Rottmühl in Oberdöbling near Vienna. The biographers of Mozart have also racked their brains on a matter concerning Perchtoldsdorf to the south of Vienna, which is known to us from the life of Hugo Wolf; Mozart sent his son Karl there, not to "a foster home" and "to strangers" but to the respectable boys' school of Wenzel Bernhard Heeger, whose name he wrote as Hecker.

One very curious error resulted from a misplaced comma. Marianne Kirchgässner, the blind virtuoso on the glass harmonica, gave three concerts in 1791; the second of these, which took place on the 19th of August in the Kärntnertor Theater, was advertised in the *Wiener Zeitung* on the 13th and 17th. There it was set forth that she would play among other things "a completely new and exceedingly beautiful Quintet with wind accompaniment, by the Kapellmeister Mozart [ein ganz neues, überaus schönes Konzertquintett mit blasenden Instrumenten begleitet, von Herrn Kapellmeister Mozart]." Abert puts the comma before "begleitet," altering the meaning to "a . . . quintet with winds, accompanied by the Kapellmeister Mozart." Since then, many researchers have puzzled over the problem of which instrument was played by Mozart in the Adagio and Rondo for Glass Harmonica, Flute, Oboe, Viola, and 'Cello. (Let it be remarked in passing that Abert also misdates the concert, putting it in June, and that he calls the piece a "Konzertantquintett.")

The history of *Die Zauberflöte* brings with it a whole series of errors. Ironically, the man who has written most about it, namely Egon Komorzynski, recently has erred the most. After the publication of his first book, a good one on Emanuel Schikaneder (1901), but before his later work, a number of legends persisted: that the Theater auf der Wieden, also called the Freihaus Theater, was a very small wooden structure, that Karl Ludwig Gieseke was to be regarded as the real author of the text of *The Magic Flute,* and that the character of Sarastro was a glorification of Ignaz von Born, the spiritual leader of the Viennese Freemasons, although Born had withdrawn from the order in 1786. In 1941 Komorzynski published in Berlin a novel entitled *Pamina,* a tribute to Anna Gottlieb, who at twelve was the first Barbarina and at seventeen the first Pamina. At the same time there appeared his biography of Mozart, which was published in revised form in 1955, while in 1951 appeared the third edition of his book on Schikaneder, significantly enlarged though still incomplete in its documentation. (This work was reprinted under a new title in 1955.) *Hinc illae lacrimae.* The following is only a sampling from these two biographies of those hypotheses which through frequent repetition have grown into theses and have already been widely adopted by other authors. These two books, which themselves appropriate from other authors several errors long since corrected, present a peculiar blend of novel and biography, with fact and invention often intermingled in the same sentence. For example, it is true that Beaumarchais's comedy *Le mariage de Figaro* was to have been given by Schikaneder's company at the Vienna Burgtheater on February 3 (not 4), 1785, but was not performed because Emperor Joseph II forbade it. Komorzynski now ascribes to Schikaneder the translation that was permitted to be published and lists it among his works. Actually, however, it was the work of Johann Rautenstrauch. But we shall limit ourselves to *The Magic Flute*. Emil Karl Blümml, Roland Tenschert, and Alfred Einstein have long since established that Gebler's play *König Thamos* was first given in Salzburg by Karl Wahr's company on January 3, 1776, though the music evidently was not Mozart's. (Alfred Orel has recently discovered that two choruses from Mozart's music for *König Thamos* were sung as early as April 4, 1774, at the performance in the Vienna Kärntnertor Theater.) Then, during the season of 1779-80 Josef Böhm's company gave the play again in Salzburg, with Mozart's complete music. The play is not found in Schikaneder's Salzburg repertory of 1780. Nevertheless, Komorzynski retains the old legend that Schikaneder performed it in Salzburg at that time with all of Mozart's music; now he avers that Schikaneder and Mozart decided on the spot to write a German opera and that the name Tamino obviously was derived from Thamos. Through a manifold misunderstanding of an entry in the marriage register of the parish church of the Paulist fathers near the Freihaus, Komorzynski has concluded that the first Sarastro, played by a staff composer attached to Schikaneder's troupe, was not Franz Xaver Gerl but his younger brother Thaddäus, who was, to be sure, also a chorister in Salzburg but who never belonged to a theatrical company. During the last conference on Mozart in Salzburg, Alfred Orel refuted this hypothesis of Komorzynski in detail. The worst consequences of this author's imagination are revealed, however, in the portrayals of Anna Gottlieb in biographies, novels, and recently in a film. Komorzynski, fondly calling her Annerl (her pet name was in fact Nanette) presents her as Mozart's favorite pupil and his beloved, the Muse of his last years, who stopped singing when he died. As far as we know, Mozart never taught singing; moreover, he was closer than ever to his wife during his last year. As for Anna Gottlieb, she was a successful singer and actress at the Theater in der Leopoldstadt for many years after 1791.

The little note supposed to have been written by Schikaneder to Mozart in 1790 concerning the duet of Papageno and Papagena has long been recognized as a forgery, yet this letter is still used as evidence that the composition of *The Magic Flute* had already begun in that year.

But probably the best story of all about *The Magic Flute* is the newest. In the Mozart number of the Freemasons' magazine *Alpina* (Bern, January 1956) the music critic Gustav Renker published a serious article called "Mozart and Our Time." Using as his source Ernst Lothar's novel *Der Engel mit der Posaune* (first published in 1946 as *The Angel with the Trumpet,* Cambridge, Mass.), he cites a complaint to the Vienna prefecture of police dated September 2, 1791. The anonymous author of this document charges that on the previous evening in the new quarters of the Vienna lodge "Zur Zukunft" Schikaneder outlined the opera to the brothers and Mozart, in a pitiable condition, sang and played his unmelodious new work. This complaint, along with other fabricated documents, stands at the beginning of this novel, where it is stated that the Viennese police after an investigation tabled the affair. On the evening of September 1 Mozart was still in Prague; furthermore, there was no lodge "Zur Zukunft" nor any other lodge at the place named in the novel. Still, the credulous interpreter of the novel seeks to soothe us with the words: "Today one can smile over such judgments." Smile? One can laugh.

*(Translated by Christopher Hatch)*

# NORTON PAPERBACKS ON MUSIC